The Passion of Barbeque

The Passion of Barbeque

Presented by
The Kansas City Barbeque Society

New York

Responsibility for the success and/or originality of the recipes contained herein rests with the Kansas City Barbeque Society.
Editor: Jane Doyle Guthrie
Text Illustrations: Lou Copt
Cover Photography: Glen Wans
Ribs courtesy of K.C. Masterpiece Restaurant & Grill

Library of Congress Cataloging-in-Publication Data

The Passion of barbeque / presented by the Kansas City Barbeque Society
      p.   cm.
   Originally published: Kansas City, Mo. : Pig Out Publications, 1989.
   Includes indexes.
   ISBN 1-56282-965-3 : $10.95
   1. Barbeque cookery—Missouri—Kansas City.   2. Kansas City
Barbeque Society.   I. Kansas City Barbeque Society.
TX840.B3P37   1992
641.5′784—dc20   92-12
                                                                 CIP

FIRST EDITION

10 9 8 7 6 5 4

Contents

Two Bone Section *"A Well-Spent Afternoon"* 51

Acknowledgments

The Passion of Barbeque is a presentation of award-winning recipes and barbeque cooking techniques collected from the Kansas City Barbeque Society. As with any undertaking, certain individuals make essential contributions and it is here that we acknowledge them.

The initial impetus, from dream to reality, began with Rick Welch, who gathered the key players and "sparked" the fire. Bruce Daniel transcribed the barbeque techniques contained here with tantalizing style, embodying the word PASSION. Carolyn Wells, as administrator of the Kansas City Barbeque Society, compiled the pertinent Society information for the book. And competent professionals edited, typeset, and printed the final result.

Special thanks go to all KCBS members who have promoted *The Passion of Barbeque,* the first-ever barbeque society cookbook. Final recognition and thanks are extended to the following members who contributed the recipes (many of them award winners) for this superb grilling and smoking collection:

Karen Adler	Dan Haake	Paul Schroeger
Matt Bilardo	Jessica Kirk	Guy Simpson
Rita Barber Cucchairra	Paul Kirk	Alan Uhl
Bill Brown	Al Lawson	Harold T. Walker
Tom Bryon	Donna McClure	Rick Welch
Bruce Daniel	Janeyce Michel	Carolyn Wells
Charla Daniel	Mark Mooney	Gary Wells
Ar'die Davis	Karen Putman	
Rich Davis	Mark Schroeger	

Preface

The Passion of Barbeque has been created to serve a noble, two-fold purpose: to involve as many people as possible in the activity of barbequing, and to provide the instruction and insight necessary for truly transcendental barbeque. The aim within these pages is to educate. Novices may fear failure, assuming that good barbeque is beyond their reach. Others may have reached a barbeque "comfort level," but would like to experiment a bit or vary the menu. Experienced grillers and smokers may have their technique down cold, but suspect there's something they could do better. This book addresses every level of barbequer.

Members of the Kansas City Barbeque Society maintain that the size and cost of equipment has little bearing on the ultimate quality of food produced. Further, novice and professional can benefit from the shared knowledge this book brings together. Once exposed to the diverse flavor possibilities of *true* barbeque, the reader-chef starts down a glorious road, the search for the combinations of flavor and technique that taste and "feel" best. And what better way to experiment than to take advantage of the accumulated knowledge of the most advanced barbeque group in the world—the Kansas City Barbeque Society.

This book is organized by "The Bone System," which groups recipes by the amount of time involved during the barbequing process. Often cookbooks or food books put all the pork or all the poultry together, with the tough stuff next to easy things that take fifteen minutes; an entire section has to be scanned to sort out possibilities. Not so in *The Passion of Barbeque*.

The One Bone section contains meat, poultry, and seafood recipes that take from fifteen minutes to an hour. These are primarily grilling techniques, meant to be accomplished in a minimum of time and generally over high heat. The title for the section is "Home by Five, Barbeque by Seven," and this typifies the One Bone approach—quick preparation.

Two Bone creations ("A Well-Spent Afternoon") require more time, normally two to four hours. This group represents slower, lower temperature cooking, done in a covered unit. For those who relish an afternoon spent with friends or in the solitary reverie of the smoking ritual, plenty of inspiration awaits in the Two Bone section.

The Three Bone section title says it all: "A Smoke Marathon." These recipes need a minimum of five hours. Large cuts of meat require lots of time when slow cooking, but the rewards are great. The most ambitious of the Three Bone recipes takes twelve to fifteen hours; this section is hard-core.

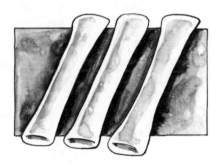

It's important to note that the recipes don't necessarily become more complex with each additional "Bone," generally just more time-consuming. And, indeed, time spent barbequing is time well spent.

The Kansas City Barbeque Society

In Kansas City, barbeque is part of the mentality. Everyone, from barkeep to corporate veep, has an informed opinion on the subject, and most can back it up on a smoker. The world's premier barbeque chefs can be found within the ranks of the KCBS—the Kansas City Barbeque Society.

In the spirit of comradery, and with the expressed desire to have a good time, the Kansas City Barbeque Society was formed in early 1986. During that initial meeting the basic barbeque philosophy was handed down: "Smoke the best barbeque possible and have fun doing it."

Of course, the Society had more in mind than philosophy. Sympathetic to the uninitiated masses beyond Kansas City who were in need of smoke education, aware of local and national contests needing quality entrants, dismayed that numerous existing competitions were vague and inconsistent in their judging criteria, the KCBS members became excited as they envisioned what could be.

Suddenly, the scope of the KCBS widened. The twelve original Society members set out on an honorable, heartfelt mission: the word must be spread worldwide that everyone is capable of impeccable barbeque. Further, they deemed it the Society's responsibility to help with everything involved in the barbeque process, from the basics of how to make a good fire, through the maze of various barbeque styles and techniques, all the way to how large competitions are best judged.

One barbeque-addled mind hit on a novel idea. To inform and educate about barbeque (and to get a jump on the traditional barbeque season), an early, closed competition dubbed "Spring Training" would be held. Open to all Society members (by then numbering 34), this initial contest focused on sharing techniques, debating what constituted prizewinning barbeque, and generating a positive atmosphere for the creation of new and wonderful kinds of barbeque. Success, success. Spring Training was a hit. The Barbeque King and Queen were crowned. Membership picked up. Board meetings (!) were held. It began to look like an organization.

Never straying from the basic goals of 1) promote the best barbeque, Kansas City Barbeque, and 2) enjoy doing it, the Society quickly ran through all the gears and hit overdrive. From a dozen founding members, the head count in 1989 was over 500, making the KCBS the largest group of its kind in the world. Many major contests began seeking official sanction by the Society and then adopting the judging criteria hammered out by its members. The administrative arm of the Society began helping with various civic and charitable causes and to date has aided in the production of over 100 local, regional, and national contests.

So who are these people? First, a word about who they're not. No one is employed by the Society. No one receives a salary or any money for winning contests. After years of backyard and competitive trial and error, these individuals have evolved barbeque to an art form. Within the KCBS lurk giants of the genre, warlords whose presence at contests makes mere mortals cringe. Winners of innumerable awards in national and regional barbeque competitions, these are Kansas City's formidable Ambassadors of Barbeque. Many have adopted a title, a persona or *nom de grille* if you will—the Baron of Barbeque, The K.C. Rib Doctor, The Sultan of Slabs, The Honorable: Sir Loin. (See "Interviews with Excellence," p. 143). For them and all the KCBS members, the time spent promoting Kansas City barbeque is a "labor of love" in its purest form, the motivation being love of barbeque. (For a roster of the KCBS membership, see p. 154.)

At the next Spring Training, 300 or so "true believers" will gather to do exactly what was done at the first Society meeting—learn and share. Welders and accountants, bankers and tree trimmers, tweed-types and couples in coveralls, nurses and dancers, pros and novices, haves and have-nots. The bond is Barbeque—what better common ground?

The Passion of Barbeque

Barbeque is primal. Basic. And in its earthiness lies its appeal. Consider that prehistoric man's greatest early discovery was fire; how long could it have been after that before he had his buddies over for barbeque? "Barbeque through the Ages" is no fluke. We respond to it because it stirs all the subconscious urges piled up over millions of years, through countless ancestors, all appreciative of a good burnt end.

Year upon year, impression upon impression, the generations change. But that basic passion, the drive to nourish ourselves, is elemental. Though it never changes, our choices do. We start with mother's milk. Soft stuff is next, then forks and knives. We load up on junk food, we go to a few fancy restaurants. We eat all kinds of things. We get "experience" and the joy and cynicism that it brings.

We've had it all, food-wise.

Yet there are people out there who toil for countless hours, over smoking grills, to create one kind of nourishment unique in technique and appeal, in flavor and appearance. *Passion* drives these people. Passion drawn out over hours, savored for its lengthy, pleasurable, full-of-promise exercise. The sweet expectation of exhilarating sensory thrills. And we're talking about food here! Barbeque!

The barbeque aficionado reaches to great lengths when going "all the way" in a contest. This can include custom-made smokers, all-night preparation and cooking, enduring hordes of well-meaning friends and locals, questionable weather, second-guessers, tough judges—all of this to have some fun and maybe, maybe win a ribbon.

Then there's the backyard barbequer. Though the equipment may not be what the "big boys" have and the likelihood of an all-night effort is pretty slim, the desire and motivation are the same. Primal passion is enticing and gratifying to both the novice and the master.

Barbeque devotees become animated in descriptions of perfect pork shoulder, shaved thin and piled high. Grown men have been moved to tears when detailing the texture and aroma, the sensual explosion, of perfectly prepared brisket. Sausage, poultry, fish—each is capable of inducing rapture; any and all, done properly, can make one swoon.

There is great danger in this quest. Passion unleashed is powerful stuff. Once exposed to the sensory deluge of true barbeque, mortals risk barbeque addiction. It starts with slight twinges. A fancy dinner party that seemed a great idea bogs

3

down under the memory of a perfectly smoked slab. A trip to a swank restaurant goes sour when thoughts of a saucy tenderloin invade the mind. (Did a whiff of hickory slip in here?)

Signs of addiction. It gets worse. Business meetings are missed when the truant orders "just one more" side sausage. Telltale orange appears under usually clean fingernails; cuticles go bad with color. Late night trips crop up on unspecified "errands." Cold sweat forms on seeing Miss Piggy. Finally, hardware and hard wood invade the home. A favorite, well-worn seat is claimed at a local rib joint. The wondrous cycle is complete.

KCBS members know this cycle. Know and love it. Most can recount, in detail, their early experiences with the big "Q" Recent converts are thrilled with their progression through grilling and on to the hard stuff. They lament the lack of "good Q" in certain cities. Their immersion in barbeque becomes something to fall back on in troubled times. A flavorful way to pass time with friends, an exercise whose preparation and execution often become group efforts of the first magnitude.

Passion drives these people to revert to the most basic of all cooking methods—meat over fire—to create new and exciting flavor experiences. Passion brings them back again and again, a passion as real as its cousin, romance. Let the passion inspire you.

Barbeque Basics

Grilling and Smoking: Two Different Things

Many people have notions about outdoor cooking that lead them astray. "Let's have barbeque," your host says, as he proceeds to torch an unsuspecting chicken over an open flame, two inches above white-hot coals. First, he doesn't appreciate the not-too-subtle difference between grilling and smoking. Second, he clearly hasn't read this book.

When *grilling,* the fire's hot, things are cooking rapidly, and the need to impart smoke flavor is secondary.

Smoking is done in a covered unit; the temperature is lower, moisture is abundant, and smoke flavor is desired.

Both methods, of course, have merit. Grilling or smoking, the basic equipment is essentially the same. A covered unit makes most sense because it can be used for both types of cooking. Ideally, the unit should have vents for good air flow, a water/drip pan to keep things moist, and the flexibility to double as smoker or griller. Of course, as you progress in the art of barbeque, you'll probably end up with two pieces of equipment—a small one for grilling and a larger unit for smoking.

Control of the Basic Elements of Barbeque

If newcomers to barbeque do one thing wrong, it's usually either incinerating things on a grill or pulling underdone cuts out of a smoker. Why? Control of the elements. Assuming a covered smoker/grill, let's construct a typical scenario, including the proper construction of a fire, the possible placement of the items to be cooked, the ways of imparting moisture, and the introduction of smoke flavor.

Element One: Fire. Allow charcoal briquettes to burn until they form a thin white ash, then begin the cooking process. If *grilling,* spread the coals out and place the grill three to five inches above the fire. That's it. For *smoking,* the fire should not be directly under the meat. This indirect method keeps temperatures lower and allows for drip/water pans. Set the grill as far from the fire as possible.

Element Two: Moisture. Moisture is essential to the smoking process. The necessary moisture can be produced by basting the meat or by using either a water pan or soaked wood chips/chunks.

Element Three: Woods. Smoking's not smoking without wood. Some people soak chips or chunks for placement on charcoal fires, others build their fires out of the wood itself. Either method works. The choice of wood is strictly personal. Some swear by the flavor of hickory, others are wild for pecan or apple.

Element Four: Time. From fifteen minutes to fifteen hours, barbeque recipes cover the spectrum. The time required ends up being a product of properly controlled amounts of the other elements. Translated, that means that the suggested times for any smoke recipe will be affected by the control of fire and moisture (and, of course, the outdoor conditions).

Putting it all Together

Control of barbeque's basic elements is "what it's all about," and there's a little magic in it. The right mix of fire, moisture, and time will give good results. Of course, a flavorful marinade, a terrific rub, fresh herbs, a good cut of meat, a top-flight sauce—these all help, too. KCBS members all know the value of learning this control. They spend time understanding the characteristics of their smokers, experimenting with different woods, trying different techniques.

A sample setup for smoking: in a covered unit, the grill sits well above the burning charcoal/wood chips, the meat is off to one side for indirect heat, and a water pan placed opposite the meat provides essential moisture.

As any good pit boss will tell you, once heat and humidity are controlled and maintained, excellent results are easily attained, and those results can be easily repeated. Tool-wise, there are a few "good things to have" when preparing to barbeque:

Charcoal chimney (handy for getting fires going quickly; also helps when replenishing with fresh charcoal)

Tongs

Apron (things can get messy)

Mitt or glove that can handle heat

Spray bottle of water
+ baking soda
(to douse fires that flare)

Basting brush

Veterinary syringe
(for injecting marinades into meats)

Meat thermometer

Candy thermometer
(to check smoker heat)

Wire brush

So Let's Smoke Something!

Step-by-Step Smoked Chicken Halves:

1) Mound 25-30 hardwood charcoal briquettes on one side of the fire grate in your smoker, or place the same amount in a charcoal chimney. Start the fire.
2) Allow chicken halves to reach room temperature before placing them in the smoker. (This goes for any meat to be grilled or smoked.)
3) When coals are white, add premoistened wood chunks or chips (your choice of wood). Don't spread the fire out as you would for grilling; leave it pretty well piled up on one side so that you can place the meat opposite, not above, the fire. Add a water pan, if desired.
4) Place the chicken on the grill, close the lid and set the topside vents at least half, possibly three-quarters, closed.
5) Monitor temperature in the smoker and adjust it to 200-220 degrees. Once this temperature range is reached, the only reason to open the lid is to add more briquettes and/or wood, or to baste the meat if you've decided that basting's part of the method you want to use. Add briquettes or wood when the temperature drops 20-25 degrees. Some smoke should be wafting out of the unit at all times.
6) Monitor the smoker, baste and turn the meat, add fuel as needed, and 2–2 ½ hours later, have a smoked chicken feast.

Notice that the use of a marinade, a baste, a rub, or a certain kind of wood is not spelled out in the steps described above. That's because the Magic of Barbeque lies in how *you* mix all the items other than the basics, the Elements.

One Bone Section

"Home by Five, Barbeque by Seven"

Barbequed Pork Chops

**4-6 large pork chops
barbeque seasoning
garlic salt
celery salt
paprika
K.C. Masterpiece sauce**

Rub pork chops with barbeque seasoning, add garlic salt to taste and a light sprinkling of celery salt. Sprinkle with paprika. Smoke over coals and hickory at a low heat for 20 minutes, then increase heat for 40 minutes. Baste during last 5 minutes with barbeque sauce.

Serves 4-6

One Bone **11**

Sweet 'n Sour Chops

8 pork chops (1 in. thick)
1 1/2 C. pineapple chunks
1 green pepper, cut in strips
1 onion, sliced thin
2 1/2 C. lemon-lime carbonated beverage

Sweet-Sour Sauce

3 C. pineapple juice
1 C. vinegar
1 C. brown sugar
1/4 C. butter
1/4 C. cornstarch
2 T. soy sauce
1 T. Worcestershire sauce
1/2 t. salt

Combine all sweet-sour sauce ingredients in a saucepan. Cook over low heat until clear and thickened, stirring constantly. (If desired, add pineapple, green pepper, and onion during last 4 or 5 minutes.)

Add lemon-lime beverage to 1 cup of sweet-sour sauce to make a tenderizing marinade. Pour marinade over chops, cover and chill overnight.

Broil chops over medium-hot charcoal fire for 10-12 minutes per side, turning only once. Baste chops with sauce during last 4-5 minutes of grilling time.

Serves 8

Char Siu (Chinese Sweet Roasted Pork)

2 lbs. lean pork

Marinade

1/2 C. brown sugar
2 t. hoi sin sauce
1/4 C. honey
1/2 t. five spice
1 t. salt
2 t. gin or rum
1/4 t. red food coloring
1 t. garlic powder
1/2 C. soy sauce

Cut pork into 1 1/2 x 1 1/2-inch strips. Combine meat with other ingredients and let soak for 1 hour or overnight in the refrigerator.

Drain pork. Place on a rack and bake at 350 degrees for 1 hour or barbeque on a grill.

Slice and serve either hot or cold.

Serves 4-6

Grilled Ham Slice

1 ham slice (1 1/2 in. thick)

Basting Mixture

3 T. brown sugar, packed
2 T. melted butter
1 T. lemon juice
1 T. dry mustard
1 t. orange peel
dash paprika

Combine all ingredients for basting mixture. Trim outside fat from ham.

Place ham on grill, about 5 inches above coals. Brown on one side, then turn. Begin basting and cook approximately 20 minutes, turning and basting frequently.

Serves 4

Barbequed Pork Burgers *Baron of Barbeque*

2 lbs. ground pork
1/4 C. buttermilk
2 t. seasoned salt
1 t. black pepper
1/4 t. garlic powder
1/4 t. ground oregano
1/4 C. onion, minced

Combine all ingredients. Mix thoroughly and form into 1/4-pound patties.

Sear on grill, then reduce flame and cook over direct heat, about 10 minutes each side.

Serves 4-6

Guy's Quick Grilled Pork Steaks

The K.C. Rib Doctor

4 pork steaks (1/2 in. thick)
K.C. Rib Doctor Seasoning (or any barbeque seasoning)
barbeque sauce

Cover both sides of meat with seasoning.
Grill 5 inches over moderate coals for 40 minutes, turning often.
Apply sauce during last 10 minutes and continue to turn every 3
minutes to avoid burning.

Serves 4

Spicy Pork Steak

1 1/2-2 lbs. pork steak

Dry Spice Rub

1 t. garlic powder
2 t. black pepper
1/2 t. cayenne pepper
1 T. paprika
1/2 t. thyme
1/2 t. oregano
1/2 t. rosemary
1/2 t. salt

Combine dry spice rub ingredients and coat both sides of meat with barbeque seasoning. Let stand at least 30 minutes before cooking.

Grill over medium coals (225 degrees) for about 15 minutes per side, depending on thickness. Sprinkle on additional barbeque seasoning after turning meat.

Serves 4-6

Barbequed Pork Loin Baby Back Ribs

1 slab pork loin baby back ribs

Marinade

1/2 C. chicken stock
1/2 C. soy sauce
1/4 C. oil
1/4 C. vinegar
6 T. sugar
2 cloves garlic, minced

Combine marinade ingredients and marinate ribs in refrigerator from 2 hours to overnight.

Remove ribs from marinade and sprinkle with dry barbeque seasoning. Cook over medium coals (225 degrees) until internal temperature registers 160 degrees on a meat thermometer. Baste with marinade or sprinkle lightly with dry seasoning every 30 minutes during cooking process.

Serves 2-3

Barbequed Tenderloin

4 1/2 - 5 lb. pork tenderloin
salt

Marinade

3 T. soy sauce
freshly ground pepper
3 sprigs rosemary (or 1 T. dry)
2/3 C. fresh orange juice
3 cloves garlic, minced

Place meat in shallow pan and add marinade ingredients. Turn several times to mix marinade. Cover and refrigerate at least 2 hours, turning meat once or twice during that time.

Brush grill racks with oil and place tenderloin on the grill (either in smoker or over charcoal). Sprinkle lightly with salt and grill, turning once until brown and crusty (about 25-30 minutes).

Let stand 10 minutes before slicing on the diagonal, 1/2 inch thick.

Serves 8-12

Kansas City Strip Steak *Rick Welch*

2 Kansas City strip steaks
Kansas City Steak Baste (or a combination of Worcestershire
    sauce and beef broth)
1/4 C. hot water
1 3/4 T. vinegar
Kansas City Steak Seasoning (or any barbeque seasoning)

Bring steak to room temperature. Combine water and vinegar with 1 tablespoonful of steak baste and stir until dissolved. Apply baste to both sides of steak and let stand for 15 minutes.

In a covered grill, mound charcoal and ignite. Allow charcoal to burn down until completely gray. Place meat directly over fire and sear both sides. (The ideal distance between grill and top of the charcoal is 4 inches; if your grill cannot be altered, it may be necessary to adjust grilling times listed below.) Close or cover grill, but leave all air vents open.

Grilling times are based on a steak 1-inch thick; allow more time for thicker cuts:

Rare—6 minutes, flip, 3 minutes
Medium rare—8 minutes, flip, 4 minutes
Medium—8 minutes, flip, 8 minutes

Serves 2

Moon's Marinated Flank Steak

1 flank steak, trimmed

Marinade

2 cloves garlic, crushed
2 1/2 T. vinegar
1/4 C. honey
1/4 C. soy sauce
1 1/2 t. ginger
3/4 C. vegetable oil

In a glass baking dish, combine all marinade ingredients. Add flank steak and refrigerate overnight.

Grill over hot coals 4-5 minutes on each side. Thinly slice across the grain of the meat before serving.

Serves 1-2

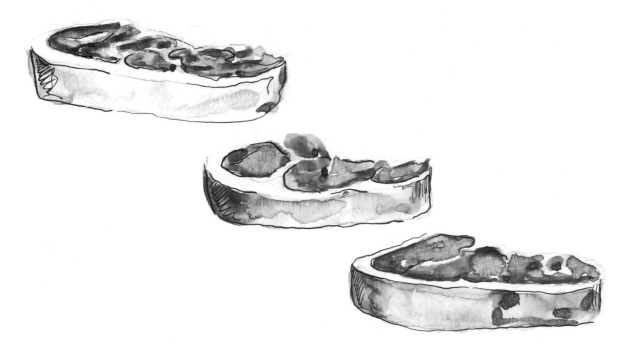

Western-Style Flank Steak

1 1/2 lbs. flank steak

Marinade

1/2 C. vegetable oil
2 T. lemon juice
1 t. Season-all
1/2 t. celery salt
1/2 t. coarsely ground black pepper
1/2 t. onion powder

Combine marinade ingredients and pour over steak in a shallow dish. Marinate 4-6 hours.

Grill 4 inches from coals for 15-20 minutes, turning once and basting often with marinade. Before serving, carve into thin slices on diagonal against the grain.

Serves 4

Barbequed Bologna Roll

**4 lb. bologna roll
whole cloves**

Sauce

**1/2 C. chili sauce
2 T. lemon juice
1 t. barbeque spice
1 t. prepared horseradish
1/2 t. dry mustard**

Mix sauce ingredients well to make a barbeque baste. Score bologna roll, cutting diagonal lines 1/8 inches deep to form a diamond pattern. Stud each diamond with a whole clove.

Place meat about 5 inches above coals. Cook 30 minutes, or until heated through, basting frequently with sauce.

Serves 8-10

Charcoal-Grilled Steak

4 club steaks (1 in. thick)

Marinade

1/2 C. vegetable oil
2 T. lemon juice
1 1/2 t. Worcestershire sauce
1 t. onion salt
1/2 t. Season-all
1/4 t. coarsely ground black pepper
1/8 t. garlic powder

Place steaks in shallow baking dish. Combine marinade ingredients and pour over meat, thoroughly coating both sides. Marinate 4-6 hours in refrigerator, turning once or twice.

Place steaks on grill and sear both sides, then raise grill to about 5 inches from coals. Cook 15 minutes, turning once, or to desired doneness.

Serves 4

Steak Teriyaki

3 lbs. round or sirloin steak (1 in. thick)

Marinade

1/2 C. soy sauce
3 T. dark brown sugar, packed
1 t. ginger
1/2 t. dry mustard
1/8 t. garlic powder
1/2 t. coarsely ground black pepper
2 t. lemon juice
1 (12 oz.) can beer
2 T. salad oil

Combine marinade ingredients and pour over steak. Cover and refrigerate 12-24 hours.

Grill 3-4 inches from hot coals, basting frequently with marinade, for about 20 minutes (10 minutes each side) or to desired doneness. Slice steak thinly on the diagonal before serving.

Serves 8-10

Guy's Calves Liver Steak *The K.C. Rib Doctor*

1 calves liver steak (1-2 in. thick)
olive oil
K.C. Rib Doctor Seasoning (or other barbeque seasoning)

Brush olive oil over steak and sprinkle barbeque seasoning over both sides.

Grill appproximately 15 minutes for a pink rareness.

Great with Sautéed Onions Barbeque Style (see recipe, p. 132).

Serves 1-2

Guy's Fuzzy Navel Steak *The K.C. Rib Doctor*

1 sirloin steak (1 in. thick)

Marinade

3/4 C. fresh orange juice (2 oranges)
1/4 C. light soy sauce
1 clove garlic, minced
1/4 t. ground clove
**1 T. K.C. Rib Doctor Seasoning (or other barbeque
    seasoning)**

Combine ingredients to make marinade. Place steak and marinade in a sealable plastic bag and keep in refrigerator 2-4 hours, turning often.

Drain off marinade and grill steak to desired doneness (16 minutes for medium), turning once.

Serves 1-2

Guy's "Poor Man" Steak *The K.C. Rib Doctor*

1 round steak (2 in. thick)

Marinade

1/2 C. light soy sauce
5 T. honey
1/4 C. cider vinegar
1 1/2 C. Italian dressing
2 green onions, chopped fine (tops included)
1 T. ground ginger
3 T. K.C. Rib Doctor Seasoning (or other barbeque seasoning)

Blend all ingredients into a marinade and cover. Trim steak and marinate for 4 hours at room temperature. Turn meat every hour.

Grill steak for 8 minutes over prepared coals, then turn and baste with marinade for 4 minutes. Repeat this process, turning and basting two more times for a total cooking time of 20 minutes, which will produce a perfect medium steak.

Let stand for 10 minutes and slice as thin as possible, diagonally across the grain.

Serves 8

Sunday Night Steak

1 sirloin steak
3 large cloves garlic, minced
freshly ground black pepper to taste
1/2 C. Italian dressing

Rub steak with garlic and pepper and let stand for 30 minutes.
Grill over medium coals to desired doneness, turning once.

Serves 2

Charbroiled Steaks *Baron of Barbeque*

4 Kansas City strip steaks (2 in. thick)
1/4 lb. butter, softened but not melted
3 large cloves garlic, minced

Combine butter and garlic and rub on steaks.
Sear meat over hot flame, then grill 8 minutes on each side to produce a medium-rare steak.

Serves 4-6

Smokey Wind Lamb Kebab

3 lbs. lamb, cubed
green peppers
sweet red peppers
onions

Marinade

3/4 C. olive oil
1 clove garlic, minced
1/2 t. oregano
1 T. soy sauce
1 T. mint
pinch allspice

Combine marinade ingredients and marinate lamb cubes overnight.

Cut peppers and onions into slices the same size as lamb cubes. Arrange on skewers, alternating peppers, lamb, and onion. Using charcoal briquettes and hard wood, grill covered over direct heat for 30-45 minutes, turning four times. (Adjust cooking time to temperature of grill; do not overcook.)

Serves 6-8

Barbequed Lamb Steaks

6 lamb steaks (about 1 in. thick)

Marinade

1/2 C. oil
1/2 C. dry white wine
1/2 t. sage
1/4 t. pepper
1/2 C. wine vinegar
1 clove garlic
1 t. salt

Lamb Steak Salsa

2 (14 oz.) cans tomatoes, chopped
3/4 C. onion, chopped
1 C. green pepper, chopped
1 t. vinegar
1 t. Worcestershire sauce
1/2 C. chopped celery
1 1/2 t. salt
1 t. horseradish
1 t. sugar
1 pickled jalapeno (optional)

Combine marinade ingredients. Add lamb and marinate in refrigerator for 24-36 hours.

Mix together salsa ingredients (pickled jalapeno will make mixture hot) and refrigerate overnight.

Drain lamb and grill above hot coals for 12 minutes, then turn and grill an additional 12 minutes (or until done as desired). Do not overcook; meat should be slightly pink on the inside (so flavor will not be gamey or strong).

Serve with salsa.

Serves 6-8

Marinated Veal Steak

2 lbs. veal steak (1 in. thick)

Marinade

1 (8 oz.) can tomato sauce
1/4 C. salad oil
1/4 C. dry white wine
1 t. oregano
1/2 t. garlic salt
1/4 t. black pepper
dash ground cloves

Mix marinade ingredients and pour over steak in glass or enamel dish. Refrigerate for 24 hours, turning meat occasionally.

Grill steak 3-4 inches from coals, 5-8 minutes on each side or to desired degree of doneness.

Serves 4-6

Easy Barbeque Chicken

1 chicken fryer, cut up
vegetable oil
Dry Poultry Seasoning (see recipe, p. 102)

Moisten chicken pieces with oil, then sprinkle liberally with barbeque seasoning.

Cook on grill 40-60 minutes, adding seasoning as chicken pieces are turned.

Serves 2-3

Grilled Spicy Lemon Chicken

1 chicken fryer, cut up
2-3 T. butter
juice of 2 lemons
Italian dressing

Mix lemon juice and butter with Italian dressing. Marinate chicken in a bowl or a sealable plastic bag under refrigeration for at least 20 minutes or up to 2 hours.

Grill chicken over medium to hot coals, basting with marinade mixture every 10 minutes.

Serves 2-3

The Baron's Barbeque Chicken

Baron of Barbeque

2 whole chicken fryers, cut in half
2 T. garlic salt
1 T. paprika
1 T. black pepper

Baste

1 C. water
1 C. catsup
1/4 C. cider vinegar
2 T. instant onions
3 T. Worcestershire sauce
1 t. dry mustard

Mix garlic salt, paprika, and pepper. Sprinkle over chicken, covering the entire surface.

Place chicken on the grill skin-side up over a medium-hot fire. Cover and grill for 30 minutes; turn and cook another 15 minutes.

While chicken is grilling, make a baste by stirring together the remaining ingredients in a small saucepan. Bring mixture to a boil, then turn down heat and simmer for 10 minutes.

When chicken is tender, baste entire surface and cook for another 5 minutes; turn and baste again. Chicken is done when it has a good glaze on it (be careful not to burn).

Serves 4-6

Grilled Lemon Chicken

2 1/2-3 lb. chicken fryer, cut up

Marinade

1/4 C. soy sauce
2 T. dry white wine
2 T. lemon juice
1/2 t. hot pepper sauce
2 green onions, finely chopped
1 clove garlic, crushed

Combine marinade ingredients and marinate meat for 6-8 hours.
Grill chicken for 20-30 minutes until done.

Serves 3-4

Famous Kansas Flightless Chicken Wings

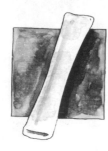

3 lbs. chicken wings
1/2 C. Dijon mustard
2 t. olive oil
4 cloves garlic, minced
1/4 C. soy sauce
1/2 t. ground ginger

Cut chicken wings into three pieces and discard the tips. Combine other ingredients in a large bowl. Add wing pieces and stir to coat well. Cover and let stand for 45 minutes.

Place wing pieces on the grill and brush with remaining mustard mixture. Grill over medium-hot coals about 15-20 minutes, turning once.

Serves 6-8

Mooney's Grilled Teriyaki Chicken Salad

4 large chicken breasts
celery
mayonnaise
lemon pepper to taste

Marinade

4-6 cloves garlic, sliced
1/2 C. soy sauce
1/4 C. sake or dry sherry
2 T. sugar
2 t. dry mustard

Clean chicken breasts thoroughly. In a glass dish, combine marinade ingredients. Add chicken to this mixture and refrigerate 4-6 hours, turning several times.

Grill over medium coals for approximately 35-45 minutes. (It's okay if skin becomes blackened, but don't allow chicken to overcook and become dry.)

Remove chicken from heat and allow to cool. Skin and debone the breasts, then coarsely chop the meat. In a bowl, combine chopped chicken, celery, mayonnaise, and lemon pepper.

Serve on lettuce plate with sliced tomatoes and hardtack or good-quality wheat crackers. Garnish with lemon wedge and fresh dill weed.

Serves 4

Guy's Chicken Wings   *The K.C. Rib Doctor*

1 lb. chicken wings

Marinade

5 T. soy sauce
5 T. lemon juice
1 T. honey
2 T. catsup
4 T. K.C. Rib Doctor Seasoning (or any barbeque seasoning)

Divide each wing into two parts at the joint. Mix marinade ingredients in a bowl, then add wings and coat well. Marinate for 2 hours.

Cook wings over prepared coals for 15 minutes, then turn and brush on remaining marinade. Continue cooking for 15 minutes. (Due to honey coating, watch wings carefully—they are easily burned.)

Serves 4

Citrus-Buttered Lobster Tails

4 frozen lobster tails
1/4 C. butter or margarine, melted
1 T. lemon juice
1 t. orange peel, finely grated
1/4 t. salt
dash ground ginger
dash paprika

Partially thaw lobster tails. Using a sharp knife, cut down the center of the shell, through the meat but not through the undershell. Spread tail open, butterfly style.

Combine melted butter, lemon juice, orange peel, salt, ginger, and paprika. Brush mixture over lobsters.

Place tails on foil on the grill, underside down. Grill 15-20 minutes or until meat loses its translucency and can be flaked easily.

Loosen meat from shell by inserting a fork between shell and meat, then brush with butter mixture before serving.

Serves 4

Marinated Shrimp Barbeque

3 lbs. cleaned, shelled shrimp (tails left on)

Marinade

3 cloves garlic, minced
1/4 C. lemon juice
1/4 C. oil
1 t. parsley, minced
3 t. soy sauce
1 t. Louisiana hot pepper sauce
1 t. celery seed
1 C. pineapple juice
1 t. salt

Combine marinade ingredients and mix well. Marinate shrimp in refrigerator for 2-3 hours.

Shrimp are best placed in a grill basket for quick and easy turning. Cook over hot fire for 3-5 minutes on each side.

Serves 4-6

Shrimp with Seafood Butter Sauce

2 lbs. jumbo shrimp, unshelled (tails left on)
cooked long grain rice
melted butter

Marinade

1 C. olive oil
1 C. dry sherry
1 C. soy sauce
1 clove garlic, minced

Seafood Butter Sauce

1/4 lb. of butter
1 T. lemon juice
1/4 t. salt
1 T. Worcestershire sauce
1/2 T. soy sauce
1/8 t. (or 3 dashes) Tabasco sauce

Combine all marinade ingredients and marinate shrimp approximately 45 minutes.

Combine and melt sauce ingredients in a pan. Keep warm, stirring occasionally.

Grill shrimp on a skewer for 10 minutes. Serve on a bed of rice with melted butter on the side.

Serves 4-6

Barbequed Shrimp

2 lbs. jumbo shrimp
1/2 lb. butter, melted
2-3 cloves garlic, minced

Marinade

16 oz. barbeque sauce
1/2 C. (or more) apple cider vinegar

   Combine marinade ingredients and marinate shrimp (peeled, deveined, and butterflied) for 1 hour.

   Mix 1 cup of marinade with melted butter and add garlic to taste. Dip shrimp in mixture and grill for 3-5 minutes, basting when turning.

   Serves 3-4

Grilled Prawns

30-40 prawns (6-8 per person)
water-soaked bamboo skewers

Marinade

1/2 lb. unsalted butter
4 green onions, minced (white and green parts)
1 clove garlic, minced
1 T. parsley, minced
1 C. Chardonnay or dry white wine
2 T. lemon juice

Spicy Peanut Sauce

1/4 C. unsalted butter
1 C. onion, minced
1 bay leaf
1/4 t. cayenne pepper
2 C. chicken stock or water
2 T. lemon juice
2 C. chunky peanut butter
1 t. salt
2 T. brown sugar

Place butter in a skillet and melt over medium heat. Lightly sauté green onions, garlic, and parsley. Remove from heat and add wine and lemon juice. Pour mixture over prawns and marinate for at least 2 hours.

To make sauce, melt butter in a medium saucepan and sauté onion and bay leaf until onion is soft. Add remaining ingredients and blend well, stirring frequently to guard against sticking. Simmer about 15 minutes.

Place prawns on skewers and grill 2-3 minutes per side. Serve with spicy peanut sauce alongside.

Serves 4-5

Barbequed Catfish

2-4 catfish fillets
barbeque seasoning
lemon pepper
1 stick butter, melted
cheesecloth
green corn husks
K.C. Masterpiece sauce

Soak green corn husks in water several hours or overnight. Season catfish with barbeque seasoning and lemon pepper to taste. Baste with butter, then wrap fillets together in a layer of cheesecloth followed by an outer layer of corn husks. Secure with string.

Smoke over low fire of hickory and charcoal for 1 hour. Unwrap and serve brushed with barbeque sauce.

Serves 2-4

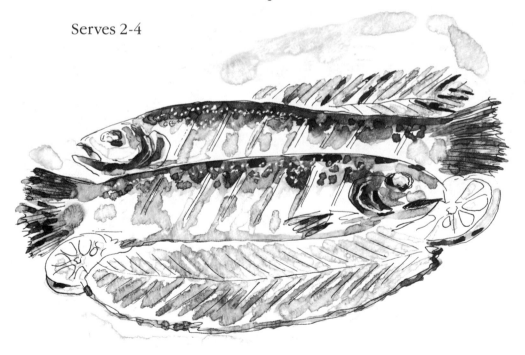

Smoked Trout

2 whole trout (1 1/2 lb. each)
paprika
seasoning salt

Marinade

1 (1/2 oz.) pkg. lemon butter
1 C. Italian dressing
1 lemon, sliced
1 onion, sliced
1 stick butter, melted

Leave trout whole with skins and heads intact; gut only. Mix marinade ingredients and pour over fish, marinating in refrigerator for 2 hours.

Stuff cavities of marinated fish with lemon and onion slices, then pour in the melted butter. Sprinkle fish with paprika and salt. Cover fish with leftover marinade, then wrap tightly in foil.

Cook on top rack of smoker for 30 minutes at 250 degrees. Open foil and cook another 5-10 minutes or until golden brown.

Remove heads from fish and peel off skin. Serve with melted butter and lemon slices.

Serves 2

Guy's Trout in a Basket *The K.C. Rib Doctor*

4 whole trout
1/2 C. all-purpose flour
1 T. K.C. Rib Doctor Seasoning (or other barbeque
   seasoning)
1/4 C. butter, melted
lemon wedges

Gut trout; remove skin and heads. In a bowl, combine flour and barbeque seasoning. Dip fish in seasoned flour, coating well, and place in well-greased wire basket.

Grill fish over hot coals about 10 minutes. Turn and baste with melted butter. Grill until fish flakes easily, about 10 more minutes. Baste often with butter. Serve with lemon wedges.

Trout can be placed directly on grill, but be very careful when turning them.

Serves 4-6

Kansas State Champion Shark

1 (12-16 oz.) shark steak per person
1/2 lb. butter
juice of one lemon
2 t. honey
5-6 fresh sweet basil leaves

Prepare a basting sauce by melting butter in a small saucepan on top of grill or smoker. Add lemon juice and honey to the melted butter, followed by basil leaves, and stir well.

Brush steak with a light coating of butter mixture and place in smoker. Leave butter mixture on top of grill and stir occasionally, basting the shark every 10 minutes while cooking.

Smoke steak for 35-45 minutes or until meat begins to pucker and surface liquid is rendered.

Serve on warm plates. Brush meat generously with remaining butter mixture, then drizzle threads of honey over the top of each steak. Garnish with additional fresh sweet basil, and place a small cup of the warm butter sauce alongside for dipping.

Each steak serves 1

Two Bone Section

"A Well-Spent Afternoon"

Barbequed Whole Tenderloin *Rich Davis*

3 large pork tenderloins (or 1 whole beef tenderloin, trimmed)

Marinade

1 C. soy sauce
1/3 C. toasted oriental sesame oil
3 large cloves garlic, minced
1 T. ground ginger
1 t. monosodium glutamate (optional)

Sauce

1 (19 oz.) bottle K.C. Masterpiece sauce, any label
1/3 C. soy sauce
1/4 toasted oriental sesame oil
1 large clove garlic, finely minced

Bring meat to room temperature. In a small bowl, mix together marinade ingredients. Pour marinade over meat in a glass or enameled pan (or use a sealable plastic bag). Cover and marinate meat overnight in refrigerator.

Place tenderloins over a low fire on a charcoal grill (with moistened hickory added to smoke). Barbeque with lid closed, turning every 15 minutes and basting with marinade, approximately 1 1/2 hours (for pork) or until done to taste (for beef).

Note: For indoor barbequing, use a 300-degree preheated oven. Follow basting directions above and cook to desired degree of doneness. (Use a meat thermometer for best results.)

Serves 6-8

Bill's Prizewinning Pork Loin

3-5 lb. pork loin
1/4 t. ground cloves
1/2 t. cinnamon
1/4 t. turmeric
1 t. salt
1/4 t. pepper
1 onion, chopped
1 C. orange juice
1/2 C. raisins
1/4 C. slivered almonds

Place roast on a double layer of foil. Mix cloves, cinnamon, turmeric, salt, and pepper and rub onto meat. Spoon chopped onion over roast.

Cook in covered grill at medium heat for about 20 minutes per pound. Then pour orange juice over meat, followed by raisins and almonds. Cook additional time until done, basting every 20 minutes. Quarter of a loin takes about 3 hours; one half a loin about 5 hours.

Amount of dry rub, onion, and orange juice may be adjusted for size of roast.

Orange Chicken: Follow recipe above, substituting one-half chicken, and cook about 2 hours total in a covered cooker or grill.

Serves 8-12

Barbequed Pork Tenderloin

1 whole pork tenderloin
Great American Barbeque and Grill Seasoning

Mix barbeque seasoning according to directions for making a marinade. Marinate meat in refrigerator overnight.

Remove pork from marinade and sprinkle with dry barbeque seasoning. Cook over medium coals (about 225 degrees) until meat registers an internal temperature of 160 degrees on a meat thermometer. Baste every 30 minutes during the cooking process.

For a tasty variation, cook the tenderloin over apple wood. It adds a lovely color, and the delicate smoke particularly complements pork. Wrap dry apple wood chips in aluminum foil and poke holes in the top. Place on the coals (this works for charcoal, gas, or electric grills). When through cooking, just throw away the foil packet.

Serves 8-10

Guy's Chinese Pork Loin   *The K.C. Rib Doctor*

2 lbs. pork tenderloin
5 T. rum
5 T. light soy sauce
3 T. K.C. Rib Doctor Seasoning (or other barbeque
   seasoning)

Combine seasoning ingredients and rub into meat. Let stand for
2 hours before cooking.

Barbeque slowly for about 1 hour. When cooled, cut into thin
slices.

Serves 6

Smoked Sausage

10 lbs. fresh pork shoulder
6 t. salt
1 t. brown sugar
1 medium clove garlic, minced
1 t. coarsely ground black pepper
1 heaping t. marjoram
1 t. paprika
1 t. parsley flakes
1 t. nutmeg
1 t. crushed red pepper
2 C. ice water
10 yds. sausage casing

Grind pork shoulder coarsely with 3/16-inch blade. Mix thoroughly with salt, brown sugar, garlic, pepper, marjoram, paprika, parsley, nutmeg, and red pepper. Add water and mix again. Cover and refrigerate overnight.

Mix ingredients again, then stuff in casings about 1 1/4 inches in diameter.

To cook, smoke 3-4 hours at 200-224 degrees.

Serves 30-40

Creole Pork Sausage

5 lbs. pork shoulder
1 medium onion, minced
2 cloves garlic, minced
1 t. paprika
1 t. crushed red peppers
1/2 t. allspice
1 t. salt
1 t. black pepper
1 t. parsley flakes
1/2 t. cayenne pepper
1/4 t. nutmeg
1 C. cold water
5 yds. sausage casing

Grind pork, using the coarse knife of a meat grinder. Add onion and garlic, then regrind. Combine remaining dry ingredients and add to meat, a little at a time. Mix thoroughly, then blend in water.

Stuff mixture into casings or make into a loaf or patties.

To cook, smoke over indirect heat for 2-2 1/2 hours.

Serves 8-12

Remus Powers' Red and White

2 (8 oz.) cans red beans (not kidney beans), drained and
   rinsed
2 (8 oz.) cans chicken broth
1 bay leaf
1 T. gumbo filé
1 medium onion, chopped
2 smoked ham hocks, with skin slit in 3 or 4 places
1 (12 oz.) bottle beer
4 cloves garlic, minced
salt and pepper to taste
2 C. long grain white rice
4 C. water
2-4 lbs. (or more) smoked sausage, cooked
chopped scallions

In a large pan, combine beans, chicken broth, bay leaf, gumbo filé, onion, ham hocks, beer, garlic, salt, and pepper. Simmer 2 hours until ham hocks are tender. Remove ham hocks and cut up, returning meat to the bean mixture and discarding skin, fat, and bones.

In a separate pan, combine rice and water. Cover, bring to a boil, then reduce heat and simmer for 20 minutes. Remove from heat and let sit, covered, another 10 minutes.

Spoon a generous portion of rice onto each plate and top with beans and bean liquor. Serve sausage on the side, garnished with chopped scallions.

Have cayenne pepper and Tabasco sauce available for folks to add as much fire as they want. Sauces such as Mister Lee's Hot and Spicy, K.C. Masterpiece Spicy, or Al Lawson's People's Choice (preferably all three) should be served with the sausage. Sourdough French bread and a cold beer will round this out into a meal you'll want at least once a week. In New Orleans, it's traditional to eat Red and White every Monday.

Serves 8-12

Mooney's Sticky Monster Bones

5-6 lbs. meaty beef ribs
1 (10 1/2 oz.) can beef broth
Dry Rib Seasoning (see recipe, p. 100)
barbeque sauce

Marinade

1 C. mesquite-flavored barbeque sauce
1/4 C. apple cider

Combine marinade ingredients. Remove membrane from underside of ribs. Place meat in shallow pan or dish and marinate 4-6 hours or overnight (refrigerated and covered).

Set up grill for indirect cooking; use several large chunks of hickory wood. Pour beef broth into drip pan, adding 1/2 cup of water if desired.

Remove ribs from marinade and drain, then liberally apply barbeque seasoning. Place ribs on grill over drip pan and smoke 2-1/2 to 3-1/2 hours, adding to the fire as needed. Mop ribs with barbeque sauce at least two to three times during final hour. Bones will hold nicely in low (200-degree) oven for several hours, covered.

Serve with extra sauce, dirty rice, or Moonman's Sweet Potato Cornbread Muffins (see recipe, p. 137).

Serves 2-3

Smoked Beef Chuck

3 lb. chuck roast, rolled and boneless

Marinade

3/4 C. wine vinegar
1/2 C. olive oil or salad oil
1/2 C. water
1 clove garlic, minced
1 T. Italian seasoning
1 t. salt

Pierce roast deeply with fork, all over. Mix remaining ingredients and pour over meat. Cover and refrigerate for 2 days, turning meat several times.

When ready to prepare, remove roast and save the marinade. Smoke for 2-2 1/2 hours, basting with remaining marinade.

Serves 6-8

Round Steak and Marinade

2 1/2-3 lbs. round steak

Marinade

1/2 C. onion, chopped
1/2 C. lemon juice
1/4 C. salad oil
1/2 t. salt
1/2 t. celery salt
1/2 t. pepper
1/2 t. thyme
1/2 t. leaf oregano, chopped
1/2 t. rosemary
2 cloves garlic, minced

Mix marinade ingredients. Marinate steak 4-5 hours, turning several times.

Grill over hot coals to desired doneness, basting with marinade during cooking. Cut into thin slices and serve.

Serves 4-6

Barbequed Rib Roast *Baron of Barbeque*

**7 lb. boneless rib roast
lemon pepper**

Marinade

**3 1/2 C. water
1 1/2 C. burgundy
1/2 C. red wine vinegar
1 medium onion, sliced thin
4 stalks celery, diced
2 cloves garlic, pressed
2 bay leaves, crushed**

Combine marinade ingredients in a pan and sauté until browned. Rub lemon pepper generously over roast, then place meat and marinade mixture in a large sealable plastic bag. Marinate in refrigerator for 4 hours.

Prepare fire on one side of grill. Remove roast from bag and place at opposite end of grill from the fire. Cover and cook at 150 degrees using indirect heat, 2 1/2 hours or 25 minutes per pound. Add moistened hickory chunks periodically to the fire.

Serves 14-20

Guy's Spicy Eye of Round Steak

The K.C. Rib Doctor

3 lbs. eye of round steak (beef)
1 bottle Italian dressing
5 T. K.C. Rib Doctor Seasoning (or other barbeque
**   seasoning)**
stone ground German-style mustard

Marinate meat overnight in refrigerator in a sealable plastic bag full of Italian dressing.

Remove meat from marinade and rub barbeque seasoning, followed by German-style mustard, over entire surface.

Place meat on a roasting rack in the center of the grill. Use a drip pan under the meat. Bank coals around outside edge of the pit and cook meat until a meat thermometer registers 140 degrees (about 1 hour).

Let stand 10 minutes before carving; slice thin.

Serves 6-8

Marinated Beef Brisket

6-8 lb. beef brisket

Marinade

1 C. (1/2 lb.) butter or margarine
2 large cloves garlic, minced
1/2 C. minced onion
1/4 C. catsup
1/4 C. chopped parsley
1/4 C. lemon juice
1/2 C. red wine vinegar
2 t. dry mustard
2 t. Tabasco
1/4 t. cayenne pepper
1/2 C. beer

To prepare marinade, melt butter, add garlic and onion, and cook for 10 minutes. Stir in remaining ingredients and simmer for 5 minutes. Marinade brisket in this mixture in the refrigerator overnight.

Place brisket over low coals (200-225 degrees) for 8-10 hours, basting with marinade every 30 minutes during cooking process. (May also be cooked, covered, in a 250-degree oven overnight.)

To serve, slice on the diagonal as thinly as possible.

Serves 12-20

Hal's Hot, Sweet, and Spicy Lamb

4-5 lbs. lamb riblets (pork chops can be substituted)

Sauce

**1 (16 oz.) bottle Amos and Ellen's Old Fashioned Chili Sauce
(or any chili sauce)**
1 T. garlic, minced
1/4 C. onion, minced
3/4 C. honey
1/2 C. brown sugar
4 oz. Worcestershire sauce
1 T. ground lemon peel
2-4 T. hot wine*
1 T. white pepper
1 T. cornstarch (optional)

Combine sauce ingredients in a pan. Bring to a boil over low heat and simmer for 10 minutes. Cornstarch may be added during heating to thicken mixture.

Place meat on hot grill and sear both sides, then allow grill to cool to 225 degrees. Continue cooking 1 1/2-2 hours until done, basting with sauce every 20 minutes.

*To make hot wine, add 1/2 cup crushed red pepper to 1 pint red wine. Heat slowly, bringing to slow boil. Boil no longer than 5 minutes. Refrigerate a minimum of one week before using; the longer the better. Stir before using. (Substitute 1 tablespoon of hot wine for every 1/4 tablespoon of cayenne pepper in any wet sauce or marinade recipe.)

Serves 6-10

Barbequed Chicken

4-6 whole chicken fryers
garlic salt
barbeque seasoning
paprika
melted butter (or fat)
K.C. Masterpiece Original sauce

Cut chickens in half, pat dry, and season with barbeque spice and garlic salt to taste. Sprinkle lightly with paprika.

Smoke birds over hickory and charcoal about 2 hours. When meat is warm, baste every 20-30 minutes with butter or fat. During last 20 minutes baste lightly with barbeque sauce.

Serves 8-12

Melt-in-my-Mouth Chicken

2 whole frying chickens
2 t. paprika
1 t. ground black pepper
2 t. garlic salt
1/2 t. monosodium glutamate
2 sticks butter, melted
barbeque sauce

Mix dry ingredients in a bowl until well blended and place in an empty spice bottle with a sprinkle top. Clean and wash the exterior and cavities of the chickens.

Put whole birds on the grill, breasts up. Baste immediately with melted butter, then sprinkle on dry mixture liberally.

Smoke slowly at 200 degrees for at least 2 1/2 hours. While chickens are cooking, brush every 30 minutes with melted butter and juices that accumulate in the cavity. Check for doneness by gently wiggling a leg—joint will be soft and tender when the chicken is done.

Cut each chicken in half and serve immediately with warm barbecue sauce on the side.

Serves 4

Chicken with Herbs

1 whole roasting chicken (about 6 lbs.)
2 t. tarragon
1 t. oregano
1 t. paprika
1/4 t. cayenne pepper
2 t. basil
1 t. thyme
1 t. savory
1/2 t. freshly ground black pepper
olive oil
4 bay leaves
4 cloves garlic, minced

Soak 1 1/2 cups mesquite wood chips in water for 20-30 minutes. During this time, prepare a kettle-type grill with 50 charcoal briquettes. While charcoal is heating, mix all seasonings (except for bay leaves and garlic) in a small bowl. Rinse chicken thoroughly in cold water; pat dry with paper towels.

Rub chicken generously with olive oil, inside and out. Sprinkle with spice mixture. Put garlic and bay leaves into cavity. Truss opening with trussing needle or string. Tuck wings behind body.

When briquettes are covered with a gray ash, divide evenly and push to sides of grill. Place a heavy-duty foil drip pan in center. Put chicken on grill and cook covered, adding about 8 charcoal briquettes every 40 minutes. Grll until juices run clear and internal temperature of thigh registers about 160 degrees on a meat thermometer (2-2 1/2 hours). Add a few drained mesquite chips to the coals afer the first hour of cooking, then more chips every 20 minutes thereafter.

Remove chicken to a serving platter and let rest 15 minutes before carving. Remove and discard bay leaves. Serve with assorted mustards or herb-flavored mayonnaise. Refrigerate any unused chicken immediately.

Serves 3-4

Barbequed Cornish Hens

4 Cornish hens

Marinade

2 C. orange juice
1/2 C. honey
1 t. celery salt
1/4 C. clarified butter
2 t. soy sauce

Prepare marinade and inject hens with part of the mixture. In a sealed plastic bag, let hens sit in remaining marinade (refrigerated) for at least 2 hours. Turn frequently.

Smoke hens for 3-4 hours on very low, indirect heat, using apple wood and plenty of water for moisture inside the grill. Baste with marinade every 30 minutes.

Serves 4-6

Marinated Cornish Game Hens

2 Cornish game hens

Marinade

2 t. oil
2 t. brown sugar
1 t. ginger
1/3 C. soy sauce
1 t. wine vinegar
1 clove garlic, minced

Mix marinade ingredients together and marinate birds overnight in refrigerator.

Bring heat in smoker to 200-225 degrees. Cook hens for 1-1 1/2 hours or until thigh meat is soft when squeezed.

Serves 2-4

Smoked Barbeque Turkey

1 whole turkey (about 10-12 lbs.)
1 onion, chopped
3 sticks celery, chopped
1 apple, wedged
vegetable oil
Dry Poultry Seasoning (see recipe, p. 102)

Baste

2 C. chicken broth
1/2 C. soy sauce

Wash bird, remove giblets, and pat dry with paper towels. Stuff cavity with onion, celery, and apple. Rub skin with vegetable oil and coat with barbeque seasoning.

Place turkey on grill and cook over medium coals (225 degrees) up to 45 minutes per pound. Baste every 30 minutes with Wicker's.

For additional smoke flavor, make an aluminum foil pouch filled with grape wood chips. Poke holes in the pouch and place over coals. This adds a delicious delicate smoke that complements the fowl.

Serves 6-10

Smoked Stuffed Flounder

2 flounder, dressed (1-1 1/4 lbs. each, heads and tails left on)
1/4 C. butter or margarine
1 1/2 C. soft bread crumbs
2 T. butter or margarine
1/2 C. green onions, chopped
1/2 C. celery, chopped
1/2 C. green pepper, chopped
2 cloves garlic, minced
8 oz. shrimp (fresh or frozen), cooked, shelled, and coarsely
**   chopped**
6-8 oz. fresh crab meat, chopped
2 T. snipped parsley
1/4 t. salt
1/4 t. ground red pepper
1/4 t. ground black pepper
2 T. butter or margarine, melted (for basting)
lime slices (optional)
green onion (optional)

In a 10-inch skillet, cook bread crumbs in 1/4 cup butter over medium heat until golden brown and crisp. Remove crumbs to mixing bowl.

In same skillet, melt 2 tablespoons butter. Add green onions, celery, green pepper, and garlic. Cook over medium heat until vegetables are tender. Add vegetables to bowl of bread crumbs, then stir in chopped shrimp, crab, parsley, salt, red pepper, and black pepper.

Rinse flounder and pat dry. To cut a pocket for stuffing, place flounder on a board, dark side up. Make a slit in the center of the fish, cutting lengthwise along backbone. Cut a pocket on both sides of first cut. Stuff pocket loosely with bread mixture.

Smoke for 2 1/2 hours, basting occasionally with melted butter. Garnish with lime slices and green onion.

Serves 2

Three Bone Section

"A Smoke Marathon"

Smokey Wind Stuffed Pork Crown Roast

1 7-8 lb. crown roast
3 green onions, chopped
4 mushrooms, diced
2 cooking apples, chopped
3 C. stuffing mix
1 C. applesauce
freshly ground black pepper

Pepper inside of roast. Sauté onions, mushrooms, and apples. Stir in stuffing mix and applesauce.

Spoon mixture into center of crown, then place roast directly on grill (away from direct heat). Smoke slowly until meat reaches 150-170 degrees. Cooking time approximately 6-8 hours.

Be creative with stuffing and you can change the flavor of the pork.

Serves 10-16

Smokey Wind Pork Spare Ribs

 **6 small slabs spare ribs**
Marinade and Baste for Pork (see recipe, p. 98)
applesauce
honey

Remove membrane from back of ribs. Refrigerate ribs overnight in marinade.

Stack ribs 6 high and cook away from direct heat, turning every 45 minutes (bottom to top). Keep a small amount of wood burning during cooking cycle (hickory, apple, cherry). At the fourth rotation, spoon a small amount of applesauce onto each slab, continuing to cook. Finish off with honey.

Ribs are finished when meat starts to pull away from bones.

Fresh meat, slow smoking, flavored steam, and not overcooking are the elements of success with this recipe.

Serves 8-12

Hal's Hot and Sweet Ribs

 **5-7 lbs. country-style pork ribs**
Hal's Hot and Sweet Sauce (see recipe, p. 104)

Smoke ribs at 225-250 degrees for 8 to 10 hours. Maintain water pan in cooker the entire time. Coat ribs with sauce on upright side every 20 minutes during final 2 hours of cooking.

Remove meat from smoker when glazed in appearance.

Serves 4-6

Three-Pepper Pork

 **1 whole pork tenderloin or boneless pork loin roast**
1/2 C. paprika
1 t. chili powder
1/2 t. cayenne pepper
water

In a bowl, mix paprika, chili powder, and cayenne pepper with a fork until blended.

Wash roast and leave wet. Rub pepper mixture generously over meat, using extra water to make the rub a thick paste. (The rub is actually fairly mild and will complement your favorite sauce.)

When your hands and the pork are bright red, put the meat on the grill and smoke it the way you know best.

Serves 8-12

Smoked Pork Tenderloin

1 whole pork tenderloin
2 C. Barbeque Rub (see recipe, p. 100)
honey
barbeque sauce

Cut tenderloin in two and wrap. Combine barbeque rub and sprinkle generously on meat. Let stand at least 4 hours in refrigerator. Remove and bring to room temperature.

Sprinkle with additional rub and place in smoker. Smoke at 200-225 degrees for 8 to 10 hours or until done. Begin basting meat with honey 4 hours before cooking is complete. Continue every 30 minutes for the next 3 hours. During last hour of cooking, baste with barbeque sauce every 20 to 30 minutes.

Let meat cool before slicing and serve with barbeque sauce.

Serves 8-12

Barbequed Whole Hog *Baron of Barbeque*

75-85 lb. hog
olive oil or vegetable oil
salt and pepper
apple (optional)
2 gal. barbeque baste

Assuming you have a smoker big enough to cook a hog, allow 2 weeks to a month lead time with your butcher. Gather plenty of wood and charcoal.

Wash hog inside and out. Trim away any loose skin or fat. Remove the kidneys. Pry the mouth open and insert a short log (to be replaced with an apple later on).

Start with the fire at about 350 degrees. While it's burning down, rub pig with oil inside and out. Rub the cavity with salt and pepper.

Find the tenderloins (in the inside from the rear end to about the middle of the pig) and cover with aluminum foil; hold foil in place with toothpicks. Then wrap the ears, feet, and snout in foil.

Place pig in the smoker with the front end close to the heat. Smoke this way for 5 or 6 hours, or until the shoulders reach an internal temperature of 90-100 degrees. Turn the pig and mop generously with baste. Check the temperature of the meat as often as possible. When the hams reach 110-120 degrees, remove foil so the ears and snout will brown.

Pork is done when internal temperature reaches 165 degrees; it should take about 12-15 hours to cook thoroughly. (Be more concerned about undercooking then overcooking.)

Serves 50-75

Barbequed Brisket

6-8 lbs. beef brisket
1/2 C. Dry Rib Seasoning (see recipe, p. 100)
barbeque sauce

Rub seasoning over brisket, then refrigerate overnight.

Place meat fat side up on grill or smoker. Cook covered at 250 degrees for 8-10 hours. Baste often with mop. Brush on favorite barbeque sauce during last 30 minutes of cooking.

Serves 8-12

Smoked Rolled Rump Roast

6 lbs. rolled rump roast

Marinade

2 C. water
2 C. vinegar
1/4 C. dried minced onion
1 lemon, thinly sliced
12 whole cloves
10 peppercorns
4 whole allspice
3 bay leaves
3 t. Season-all

Tie roast securely. Combine other ingredients, mixing well, and pour over roast. Marinate for several hours, turning meat several times.

Smoke for 4-6 hours. Carve into thin slices before serving.

Serves 8-10

Marinated Smoked Flank Steak

 **3-5 lbs. flank steak**

Marinade

1 qt. Coca-Cola
2 C. oil
2 C. vinegar
6 cloves garlic
salt and pepper to taste

Prepare marinade and marinate meat in refrigerator overnight. Remove steak from marinade and smoke at 200 degrees for 6-8 hours, basting every 20-30 minutes with remaining marinade.

Serves 6-8

Smoked Stuffed Leg of Lamb

6-7 lb. leg of lamb (about 4 lbs. after boning and trimming)
2 large bunches spinach
3 T. olive oil
2 large cloves garlic, minced
1/2 C. fresh bread crumbs
1/4 C. raisins
1/4 C. pine nuts
1/4 C. fresh chopped basil or 1 T. dried leaf basil, crumbled
2 oz. goat cheese or cream cheese, room temperature
1/2 t. salt
1/4 t. freshly ground black pepper

Bone, trim, and butterfly leg of lamb.

Wash spinach leaves and remove stems; dry with paper towels. Stack 10-12 leaves on top of each other, then roll lengthwise, jelly-roll style. Cut crosswise into 1/8-inch shreds. Repeat with remaining leaves.

In a medium skillet, heat olive oil over high heat; stir in spinach and garlic. Tossing and stirring often, cook for 2 minutes or until most of liquid has evaporated.

Spoon spinach mixture into a medium bowl and stir in bread crumbs, raisins, pine nuts, basil, cheese, salt, and pepper. Spread lamb with spinach mixture and roll up, jelly-roll style, beginning from a long side. With heavy string, tie rolled lamb at 1-inch intervals.

Smoke for 5-6 hours.

Serves 6-8

Smoked Leg of Lamb

5-6 lb. leg of lamb

Marinade

2 C. dry red wine
1 t. salt
1 t. dried oregano
1 t. dried thyme
2 t. coarse pepper
1/4 C. onion, chopped
1/4 C. parsley, chopped
3 t. soy sauce
2 t. lemon juice

Barbeque Lamb Sauce

1/2 jar red currant jelly
1 C. barbeque sauce (fairly hot)
4 t. mint jelly

Combine wine, salt, oregano, thyme, and pepper. Stir in onion, parsley, soy sauce, and lemon juice. Bone leg of lamb and place in a sealable plastic bag with marinade mixture. Marinate at least 1 hour at room temperature or overnight in refrigerator, turning occasionally. Remove lamb from marinade, roll and tie.

Roast lamb over medium coals to desired doneness (175 degrees internal temperature, still slightly pink in center). If using charcoal, add damp hickory or apple chips to coals.

To make sauce, combine all ingredients in a pan and simmer for about 15 minutes. Serve warm with lamb.

Serves 8-12

Smoked Stuffed Veal

8 lbs. veal
1 lb. ground veal
4 oz. pork fat
4 eggs
3 oz. fresh bread crumbs
16 oz. spinach, blanched, drained, and chopped
3 T. parsley, chopped
40 pitted dates, quartered
4 oz. blanched dry apples, chopped
4 oz. onions, chopped
4 oz. bacon, diced
2 cloves garlic, minced
1/2 C. green onions, chopped
1/2 t. basil
1/2 t. marjoram
1/2 t. rosemary
salt and pepper to taste

Pound out veal to 1 inch thick.

Using fine blade of grinder, grind together ground veal and pork fat several times. Chill.

Combine eggs, bread crumbs, spinach, parsley, dates, and apples. Add to ground veal mixture.

Sauté onions, bacon, garlic, and green onions until vegetables are tender and bacon crisp. Mix basil, marjoram, rosemary, salt, and pepper and add to bacon mixture. Chill, then add to ground veal mixture.

Stuff meat by spreading veal mixture over pounded veal. Roll up, wrap in bacon slices, and smoke for 4 hours.

Serves 12-16

Grilled Chicken Halves

12 chicken halves
1 T. poultry seasoning
1 C. vegetable oil
1/2 C. butter
1 t. lemon juice
1 (12 oz.) can beer (optional)

Wash chicken in cold water and pat dry with paper towels. Rub poultry seasoning on each chicken half. Refrigerate, covered, 5 hours or more.

Combine oil, butter, lemon juice, and beer, if desired. Grill or smoke chicken, covered, about 4 hours at 250 degrees, mopping frequently with oil-lemon juice mixture.

Serves 12-16

Smoked Orange Turkey

15-20 lb. turkey
salt
orange juice

Salt cavity of turkey well and place bird on double layer of aluminum foil.

Cook in covered barbecue unit with medium indirect heat (200-220 degrees) for 5-7 hours (20-30 minutes per pound), depending on temperature and size of turkey. When turkey is about half done, pour on orange juice and baste with juice and drippings every 20 minutes.

Serves 10-15

Smoked Sausage Stuffed Duck

4-5 lbs. domestic duckling
salt

Stuffing

1/4 lb. smoked sausage or andouille, cut into 1/2-in. cubes
1/2 C. celery, finely chopped
1/2 C. apple, finely chopped
1/4 C. onion, finely chopped
1/4 t. ground red pepper
2 T. butter or margarine
4 C. plain croutons
1/4 C. chicken broth

In a medium saucepan, cook sausage, celery, apple, onion, and red pepper in butter until vegetables are tender. Remove from heat. Place croutons in a large mixing bowl. Sprinkle with sausage mixture and chicken broth. Toss lightly until well mixed, then set aside.

Rinse duck and pat dry with paper towels. Sprinkle inside of cavity with salt. Spoon some of the stuffing into the neck cavity. Fasten the neck skin securely to the back of bird with a small skewer. Lightly spoon remaining stuffing into the body. Tie legs securely to the tail. Twist wing tips under back. Prick skin all over with a fork. Smoke for 4 1/2–5 hours.

Serves 6-10

Smoked Carp à la Plank *The K.C. Rib Doctor*

3 carp (about 5 lbs.)
5 T. butter, melted
1 bottle very cheap white wine
parsley
lemon slices
12 x 2 x 4-in. plank

Place carp on plank and pour melted butter over both.

Place plank and carp in smoker for 12 hours. During the 12 hours, drink the bottle of very cheap white wine.

Remove carp and plank from smoker and garnish with lemon and parsley. Then remove carp and eat the plank.

Serves 0

Marinades, Rubs, and Sauces

Marinades are usually vinegar-based liquids designed to make meats more tender. Larger cuts of meat require overnight soaking, while smaller cuts often need only a few hours. Marinades also double as "bastes," since most are used to keep things moist during the smoking process.

Rubs are just what the name implies—dry spice combinations meant to be rubbed on the item to be grilled or smoked. Many KCBS members use both a marinade and a rub, depending on the recipe.

Sauces for some people *are* barbeque. (These are the individuals this book delivers you from—those who honestly believe that any food becomes barbeque simply by swabbing sauce on it.) In fact, sauces are a final touch to the barbequing process, and properly prepared barbeque does not always benefit from the use of sauce.

Beef Steak or Roast Marinade

1/2 C. red wine vinegar
1 t. Worcestershire sauce
1 t. dried basil
1/3 C. catsup
1 t. sugar
2 cloves garlic, minced (optional)

Combine all ingredients and mix well.

To marinate, place meat in covered container or sealable plastic bag containing mixture. Marinate in refrigerator for 6 hours.

This can be used as a marinade or to brush on meat while cooking.

Yields about 1 cup

Oriental Marinade for Flank Steak

1/2 C. soy sauce
1/2 C. honey
2 t. red wine vinegar
1 1/2 t. garlic powder
1 1/2 t. ground ginger
1 t. monosodium glutamate
1/2 C. vegetable oil
4 green onions, minced

Combine soy sauce, honey, and vinegar; mix well. Stir in garlic powder, ginger, and monosodium glutamate. Add oil and green onions.

Pour marinade over meat and marinate for 4-6 hours or overnight, turning occasionally.

Yields about 2 cups

Spicy Marinade for Flank Steak

1 qt. Italian dressing
1 C. vinegar or red wine vinegar
1/2 C. green pepper, minced
1 qt. soy sauce
1/2 C. onion, minced

Combine ingredients and pour over meat.
Marinate 6-8 hours or overnight, turning occasionally.

Yields about 2 1/2 quarts

Marinade and Baste for Pork

1 clove garlic, pressed, or 1/2 t. garlic powder
1 t. dry mustard
1/2 t. salt
1 t. ground ginger
1 t. monosodium glutamate (optional)
1/2 t. white pepper
1 C. soy sauce
1/2 C. vegetable oil
1/4 C. honey

Combine all dry ingredients and sift into soy sauce. Blend in oil and honey.
Pour mixture over pork and marinate in refrigerator for 6-8 hours or overnight. Use mixture as a baste throughout cooking process.

Yields about 2 cups

Teriyaki Sauce Marinade

1/2 C. soy sauce
1/2 C. pineapple juice
1/4 t. white pepper
1 t. ground ginger
1/4 C. brown sugar
2 t. salad oil
2 cloves garlic, pressed
2 t. dry sherry

Combine all ingredients and marinate meat in refrigerator for at least 2 hours.

Yields about 2 cups

Teriyaki Marinade for Beef, Pork, or Chicken

1 C. pineapple juice
1 C. soy sauce
1/2 C. dark brown sugar, packed
1/2 t. ginger, ground
1/2 t. garlic powder
1 t. gin or rum
2 t. cornstarch
1/2 C. cold water

In a saucepan, combine pineapple juice, soy sauce, brown sugar, ginger, garlic, and liquor. Stir well and bring to a boil. In another bowl, blend cornstarch and water, then stir into the boiling sauce and simmer for 2 minutes. Let sauce cool to room temperature.
Marinate meat in refrigerator for at least 2 hours or overnight, then broil or barbeque.

Yields about 4 cups

Dry Rib Seasoning

6 t. salt
1 t. dried lemon powder
2 1/2 t. black pepper
6 t. sugar
2 t. monosodium glutamate
1 t. paprika

Combine seasonings thoroughly. Rub into meat and refrigerate overnight before cooking.

Yields about about 1 cup

Barbeque Rub

2 C. sugar
1/4 C. paprika
2 t. chili powder
1/2 t. cayenne pepper
1/2 C. salt
2 t. black pepper
1 t. garlic powder

Combine all ingredients and use as a rub for any barbeque meat.

Yields about 3 cups

Dry Poultry Seasoning

6 t. salt
2 t. monosodium glutamate
2 t. bay leaves, ground
2 t. dry mustard
3 t. black pepper
2 t. garlic powder
1 t. paprika

Combine ingredients and mix well. Rub into poultry and refrigerate overnight before cooking.

Yields about 1 cup

The Baron's Steak Sauce

1/2 lb. beef suet (fat trimmings from brisket or steak)
1/4 lb. butter
1 C. fresh mushrooms, sliced thin
1 clove garlic, minced
1/2 C. dry white wine
2 T. A-1 Steak Sauce
1 T. Worcestershire sauce

Place suet in a large skillet and heat until 1/4 cup of grease is rendered. Remove any remaining suet and add butter, mushrooms, and garlic. Cook until mushrooms are done. Add remaining ingredients and blend in. Reduce heat and simmer for 15 minutes or until mixture starts to thicken.
Spoon over steaks or serve to the side.

Yields about 3 1/2 cups

Barbeque Sauce

2 cloves garlic, minced
1/2 C. onion, minced
2 t. butter
2 t. vegetable oil
1 C. brown sugar
2 t. Worcestershire sauce
1 t. prepared mustard
2 C. catsup
1 C. water
2 t. vinegar
2 t. A-1 Steak Sauce
1/2 t. salt

In a saucepan, sauté garlic and onion in butter and oil until soft; do not brown. Add remaining ingredients and simmer over low heat for 15-20 minutes, stirring occasionally.

For a thicker or thinner sauce, adjust water accordingly.

Yields about 6 cups

Hal's Hot and Sweet Sauce

1 pt. Amos and Ellen's Old Fashioned Chili Sauce
   (or other chili sauce)
1 (24 oz.) bottle Heinz catsup
1 C. brown sugar
1 (16 oz.) bottle Coca-Cola
4 T. black pepper
2 T. mustard (white or hot)
1 T. cinnamon
2 T. monosodium glutamate
1 T. oregano
honey (optional)

Combine ingredients and blend well; honey may be added to adjust sweetness. Refrigerate until needed.

Mixture can be used on pork ribs, tenderloin, or pork roast. (Spice combination may be used as a dry rub alone.)

Yields about 8 cups

Barbeque Sauce with Peppers

1 green pepper, chopped
2 onions, finely chopped
3 T. butter or margarine
1 C. catsup
1/4 C. white vinegar
1/4 C. lemon juice
2 T. Worcestershire sauce
2 T. brown sugar
1 T. honey mustard
1 T. prepared mustard
Tabasco sauce to taste
1 red bell pepper, diced

In a 2-quart saucepan, sauté onion and green pepper in butter until tender; do not brown. Stir in catsup, vinegar, lemon juice, Worcestershire sauce, brown sugar, and mustards, mixing well. Add Tabasco and red pepper. Bring to a boil, then lower heat and simmer uncovered for 30 minutes, stirring occasionally.

Cool and store in refrigerator.

Yields about 3 cups

Barbeque Sauce for Chicken

1/2 C. salad oil
1 C. water
2 T. onion, chopped
1 clove garlic, crushed
1 1/2 t. sugar
1 t. salt
1 t. chili powder
1 t. paprika
1 t. pepper
1/2 t. dry mustard
dash cayenne
1 t. Worcestershire sauce
1 t. hot sauce
1/4 C. lemon juice
1 C. catsup
1/4 C. steak sauce
1/2 green pepper, chopped
1 T. cider vinegar

Combine all ingredients in a saucepan and simmer for 1 hour. Brush onto grilled chicken pieces.

Yields about 3 cups

Barbeque Sauce and Baste
for Chicken and Pork

1/4 lb. butter
1 C. honey
1 C. prepared mustard
1/4 C. fresh lemon juice
1 t. salt
1 t. monosodium glutamate (optional)

Melt butter in a saucepan. Blend in honey, mustard, and lemon juice. Add salt and monosodium glutamate and mix well.

Can be used as a baste throughout the cooking process. When cooking pork roast, the honey can carmelize and turn dark.

Yields about 3 cups

Barbeque Basting Sauce
for Beef or Pork Roast

1/2 C. salad oil
1/2 C. red wine vinegar
1/2 t. monosodium glutamate
salt and pepper to taste
1/2 C. lemon juice
1/4 C. soy sauce
dash of Worcestershire sauce

Mix all ingredients and refrigerate until needed.

Yields enough for a 5-10 pound roast

Side Dishes

As great as Kansas City barbeque is, it can be strongly enhanced by complementary side dishes. Although many standards, such as baked beans, have been included in this section, these are select recipes submitted by KCBS heavyweights. The K.C. Rib Doctor and Baron of Barbeque don't put supermarket potato salad on their backyard platters and neither should you. These accompaniments round out the meal, add to its presentation, and allow for additional creativity.

Fresh Cilantro New Potato Salad *Rich Davis*

2 lbs. small red new potatoes
chicken broth (approx. 4 C.)
2 egg yolks, room temperature
1/2 t. salt
dash cayenne pepper
1 t. dried mustard
2 T. vinegar
1 C. vegetable oil
2 T. half-and-half
3 T. fresh cilantro, chopped and packed
2/3 C. sweet white onion, chopped
1/2 C. celery, minced
2 T. fresh cilantro, minced
4 hard-boiled eggs, whites chopped and yolks crumbled
seasoning salt
salt
freshly ground black pepper
paprika

Scrub potatoes and cut in half, leaving skins on. Place potatoes and enough chicken broth to cover them in a large saucepan. Bring to a low boil. Cook until potatoes are tender but not mushy, approximately 15-20 minutes. Pour off and reserve broth.

To prepare mayonnaise, whip egg yolks in a blender until foamy. Add salt and cayenne pepper. With blender running, add mustard and vinegar, then slowly add oil. When mixture is thick, add half-and-half and chopped cilantro; blend well.

Cut cooled potatoes into bite-size pieces, removing skins if preferable. Add onion, celery, minced cilantro, and egg whites. Sprinkle lightly with seasoning salt and add salt and black pepper to taste. Add mayonnaise mixture, turning gently until potatoes are coated and moist (may need a splash of reserved broth to moisten). Sprinkle with crumbled egg yolks and paprika. Refrigerate until serving.

Serves 6-8

Jean's Potato Salad

10 large red potatoes
8 hard-boiled eggs, chopped
sweet pickle relish
grated onion
4 hard-boiled eggs, sliced
paprika

Sauce

2 C. Miracle Whip
3 t. sugar
vinegar
1/2 C. prepared mustard
salt and pepper to taste
1 t. celery seed

Boil potatoes in their skins. Peel while hot and mash in a bowl. Add chopped eggs, then sweet relish and onion to taste.

Mix sauce ingredients; add only enough vinegar so sauce is neither too sweet nor too sour. (For a hot, spicy salad, substitute cayenne pepper for black pepper—a little goes a long way.) Add to potato mixture.

Garnish with egg slices and paprika.

Serves 12-15

Creamy Coleslaw

4 C. cabbage, finely shredded
1/4 C. green pepper, minced
1/2 C. sour cream
1 1/2 T. sugar
1 T. vinegar
1 t. Season-all
1/2 t. dry mustard
1/2 t. celery seed
1/4 t. ginger
dash white pepper
paprika

Combine sour cream and all seasonings except paprika. Stir cabbage and green pepper into mixture.

Refrigerate 1-2 hours, allowing flavors to blend. Sprinkle with paprika and serve.

Serves 4-6

Deb T.'s Coleslaw

4 lbs. cabbage, shredded
3 medium onions, chopped
1 C. vinegar
2 T. prepared mustard
3/4 C. sugar
1 1/2 t. celery seed
1 t. salt
1 C. vegetable oil

Combine cabbage and onions.

In a saucepan, bring to a boil vinegar, mustard, sugar, celery seed, and salt. Add oil, bring to a second boil. After mixture cools, pour over cabbage and onion combination.

Refrigerate for 12-16 hours before serving.

Serves 12-16

Kraut Salad

1 1/2 C. sugar
1 C. vinegar
1 large can sauerkraut, well drained
3/4 C. celery, chopped
3/4 C. onion, chopped
3/4 C. mixed red and green peppers, chopped

Boil sugar and vinegar. In a large bowl, combine sauerkraut, celery, onion, and peppers. Add boiled sugar and vinegar. Cover and let slaw stand 12-24 hours in refrigerator.

Serves 6-8

Rita's Surprise Salad

16 oz. cheese tortellini
2 C. Havarti cheese, shredded
1 C. raw broccoli, chopped
1 C. raw cauliflower, chopped
Italian salad dressing

Combine pasta, cheese, and vegetables in a robust Italian dressing and marinate in refrigerator overnight. Stir a few times while marinating.

Serve cold.

Serves 10-12

Vermicelli Salad

1 lb. shrimp or crab meat, cooked and rinsed
1/2 C. lemon juice
14 oz. vermicelli
1 medium red onion, chopped
1 medium green pepper, chopped
1 T. parsley, chopped
1 1/2 t. celery seed
1/2 t. oregano
1/2 t. chives, chopped
1/4 C. Italian dressing
1 C. mayonnaise
salt and pepper to taste

Marinate shrimp or crab meat in lemon juice.

Cook vermicelli in boiling water, stirring constantly. Drain and blanch with cold water. Add onion, peppers, parsley, celery seed, oregano, chives, and Italian dressing. Moisten with mayonnaise, adding more if necessary. Stir in marinated shrimp or crabmeat, then add salt and pepper to taste.

Serves 8-12

Mad Dog's Barbeque Salad

6 cloves garlic
4 anchovy fillets
1/3 C. olive oil
dash of Worcestershire sauce
1 large head romaine
1/2 lemon
1 egg, beaten
1/4 C. Parmesan cheese, grated
1 C. croutons

In a large bowl, mince the garlic, then add anchovies. Using a fork, work combination into a paste. Add olive oil and Worcestershire sauce; stir.

Break romaine into bite-size pieces and stir into garlic-anchovy mixture. Drizzle lemon over this combination. Work in raw egg, then add Parmesan and mix thoroughly. Top with croutons.

It takes quite a salad to stand up to the strong flavor of barbeque.

Serves 6-8

Monster Party Salad

1 lb. fresh mushrooms, thinly sliced
3 (6 oz.) jars marinated artichoke hearts, diced
   (reserve juice)
2 lbs. cooked chicken or turkey breast, diced
2 lbs. cooked ham, diced
2 lbs. bacon, fried and crumbled
2 lbs. cheddar cheese, grated
1 doz. hard-boiled eggs, grated
3-4 ripe avocados, diced
1 (7 3/4 oz.) can pitted black olives, thinly sliced
2 bunches radishes, thinly sliced
2 bunches green onions, thinly sliced
1 1/2 pts. cherry tomatoes, halved
5-6 heads lettuce (mixed greens)

Dressing

1 C. oil
1/3 C. wine vinegar
reserved artichoke juice (see above)
1 t. sugar
1/2 t. dry mustard
1/2 t. garlic powder
1/2 t. salad herbs
salt and pepper to taste

Preparc dressing mixture and use to marinate mushrooms and artichoke hearts for 3-4 hours.

When ready to serve, combine all remaining salad ingredients in large wooden bowl and toss with marinade mixture.

Serves 24

Maurice Salad Dressing

2 C. mayonnaise
2 t. green pepper, minced
1 t. onion, minced
4 hard-boiled eggs, mashed with a fork
1 t. Worcestershire sauce
1/2 C. vinegar
2 t. garlic salt
1/4 C. salad oil
1 t. dill

Combine all ingredients in a bowl and mix well.
Chill and serve over tossed salad greens.

Yields about 4 cups

Dijon Vinaigrette Dressing

2 C. Dijon mustard
2 1/2 C. olive oil
1/2 C. white wine vinegar
2 green onions, finely chopped
1 pimiento, finely chopped
1/2 green pepper, finely chopped
5 sprigs parsley, finely chopped (optional)

Put mustard, oil, and vinegar in a blender and mix well. Pour mixture into a bowl and add remaining ingredients.

Blend well and serve over salad greens.

Yields about 6 cups

Dijon Roquefort Dressing

1 small clove garlic
1/2 C. white wine vinegar
1 T. fresh lemon juice
4 anchovy fillets, drained
1 t. dried leaf oregano or 2 1/2 t. fresh oregano, minced
1 t. celery salt
1/2 t. salt
1 egg
1/4 C. coarsely crumbled Roquefort cheese
   (or 1 oz. bleu cheese)
1/2 t. Dijon mustard
1/2 t. sugar
3/4 C. olive oil

While motor is running in a food processor fitted with steel blade, drop garlic through feed tube and mince. Add all other ingredients except olive oil. Process until blended, about 5 seconds.

Stop machine and scrape down side of bowl. With motor running again, pour oil through feed tube in a slow, steady stream. Process until combined.

Pour mixture into a bowl; cover and refrigerate until chilled (or up to 3 days before serving). Whisk briefly if dressing separates.

Yields about 1 cup

K.C. Masterpiece Barbequed Baked Beans

Rich Davis

2 (16 oz.) cans pork and beans, drained
3/4 C. K.C. Masterpiece Original sauce
1 oz. golden raisins
1/2 C. brown sugar
1 tart apple (such as Jonathan), peeled, cored, and chopped
1 medium onion, chopped
3 strips uncooked bacon, cut in half
  (or substitute 2 T. butter or margarine)

Preheat oven to 350 degrees. Mix all ingredients except bacon in a 2-quart baking dish. Top with uncooked bacon (or butter).
Bake uncovered for 1 hour.

Serves 6-8

Rib Doctor's Baked Beans

8 oz. sliced bacon, diced
1 large onion, diced
1 large green pepper, diced
1 large red bell pepper, diced
1 C. dark brown sugar, packed
1 C. tomato-based barbeque sauce
  (hot, sweet, or hickory-flavored)
1/3 C. maple-flavored pancake syrup
1/3 C. light corn syrup
3 cans (28 oz.) pork and beans, drained
2/3 C. beer or apple juice
pulverized burned ends of grilled briskets (optional)

In a heavy skillet, fry bacon over medium heat until lightly browned. Add onion and peppers and cook 3 minutes or until vegetables are crisp-tender. Stir in sugar, barbeque sauce, and syrups. Put beans in a 12 x 6 x 3-inch foil pan. Add bacon mixture, beer, and brisket ends; stir to mix.

Grill over hickory chips for optimum smoky flavor.

Burned ends left over from barbequed brisket can be frozen and thawed for later use. When pulverized in a food processor and added to baked beans, they add a lovely smoky flavor and a slightly chewy texture to the dish.

Serves 8-12

Barbequed Beans

1 lb. bacon, cut into thirds
5 (1 lb.) cans pork and beans
2 1/4 C. brown sugar
1/4 C. Worcestershire sauce
1 large onion, chopped
1 (12 oz.) bottle catsup
1/4 C. prepared mustard
2 t. liquid smoke

Fry bacon in a 4-6 quart pot until crisp. Add onion and sauté until clear. Stir in beans, then add remaining ingredients.

Bake uncovered at 325 degrees for 3 hours or until cooked down to desired consistency.

Serves 20

Three-Bean Baked Beans

1/2 lb. bacon, diced
1/2 lb. ground beef
1 large onion, chopped
1/2 C. brown sugar
1/2 C. granulated sugar
1/4 C. catsup
1/4 C. barbeque sauce
2 t. mustard
2 t. molasses
1/2 t. chili powder
1 t. pepper
1/2 t. salt
1 (16 oz.) can butter beans
1 (16 oz.) can kidney beans
1 (31 oz.) can pork and beans

Brown bacon, beef, and onion; drain. Transfer to a baking dish and add all other ingredients.

Bake at 350 degrees for 1 hour.

Serves 8-10

Texas Cowpoke Pintos

2 lbs. dried pinto beans
1/2 lb. smoked bacon
1/4 lb. salt pork
3 Italian tomatoes or 2 medium tomatoes
3 T. ground cumin
2 T. chili powder
1 T. garlic powder or 4 cloves fresh garlic, crushed
2 large jalapeno peppers, chopped
pepper to taste
salt

Wash beans thoroughly and discard any bad ones or rocks. Place beans in pot and cover with water. Bring to a boil, then pour out water. Return beans to the pot and add enough fresh water to cover beans plus 2-3 inches (for thicker sauce, use 2 inches). Add all other ingredients except salt.

Bring mixture to a boil again, then reduce to simmer. Approximate cooking time will be about 6 hours on the stovetop or 8-10 hours in a Crockpot. Season with salt during the last hour if needed, and continue cooking until done.

These beans make wonderful frijoles refrito.

Serves 10-12

Guy's Spuds *The K.C. Rib Doctor*

6 medium russet potatoes (3 lbs.)
1/4 C. olive oil
3 T. seasoned salt
bottled buttermilk dressing

Scrub potatoes and cut lengthwise into 1/2-inch thick wedges. Place wedges in a large pan and sprinkle with oil and seasoned salt; toss to coat well.

To grill: When a full bed of charcoal is white, put potatoes directly on grill, set 4-6 inches above coals. (Put hood down quickly—coals will spurt and possibly flame when hit by oil.) Cook about 40 minutes, turning with broad, long-handled spatula every 10 minutes until potatoes are browned and tender. Mound on a serving platter around a bowl of dressing so guests can "dip their own."

To cook indoors: Arrange potatoes in a single layer on a large broiler-pan rack. Broil 4-6 inches from heat source for 10-15 minutes, turning twice until potatoes are browned and tender. (If cooking in two batches, keep first batch warm in oven while broiling the second.)

Serves 6

Potatoes au Donna

6 large potatoes, peeled and sliced
1 bunch green onions (with tops)
1 stick butter
salt and pepper

With a piece of heavy-duty foil, large enough to fold back over and seal, line a casserole dish. Alternate layers of raw potato slices with several slices of butter, salt, and pepper, finishing with a top layer of green onions.

Shake a few drops of water on top of mixture, then fold foil up and seal. Bake 350 degrees for 1 hour.

Serves 6-10

Smoked Rice Pilaf

3 oz. butter
2 oz. onion, finely chopped
1 green pepper, chopped
1 lb. uncooked rice
1 C. chicken stock, heated
1 (8 oz.) can tomatoes, chopped (with juice)
salt

Melt butter in a skillet. Add onion and peppers and sauté until onions are transparent. Add rice and sauté another 10 minutes. Stir in hot chicken stock, tomatoes, and salt.

Place skillet in the hot part of the smoker and cook until liquid is absorbed.

Serves 6-10

Broccoli with Cashews

1 large bunch fresh broccoli
2 T. minced onions
2 T. butter
1 C. sour cream
2 t. sugar
1 t. vinegar
1/2 t. poppyseeds
1/2 t. paprika
1 C. roasted cashews

Cook broccoli in water until crisp. While broccoli is cooking, sauté onions in butter. Stir in sour cream and remaining ingredients except cashews.

Layer broccoli in a buttered 1 1/2–quart baking dish and cover with sauce. Sprinkle with cashews and bake uncovered at 325 degrees for 25 minutes.

Serves 6

Sautéed Onions Barbeque Style

2-3 onions, sliced
butter to taste

Wrap sliced onions and butter in foil. Place directly on top of coals and cook approximately 15 minutes.

Serves 4-6

All Mine Casserole

2 (10 oz.) pkgs. frozen kernel corn
1 medium onion, chopped
2 T. butter
4-6 yellow squash, sliced
1 t. salt
1/2 t. garlic salt
1/4 t. ground cumin
1/4 t. pepper
2 C. sharp cheddar cheese, grated
seasoned bread crumbs tossed with melted butter

Cook and drain corn.

In a large skillet, sauté onion in butter. Add squash, cover and steam until squash is tender. Drain, then add seasonings and corn. Cover and cook 5 minutes more. Stir in cheese.

Transfer mixture to a 1 1/2-quart casserole and top with bread crumbs. Bake at 350 degrees for 25 minutes.

Serves 6-8

Eggplant Casserole

1 lb. Italian sausage
2 medium eggplants
1 C. Romano cheese, grated
1 C. mozzarella cheese, grated
1 C. Parmesan cheese, grated
1/2 t. dried oregano, crushed

Brown sausage and set aside. Peel eggplant and cut into 1/4-inch slices, then steam until crisp-tender.

Butter a 9 x 13-inch pan (to cook in oven) or heavy-duty foil (to grill). Make layers of eggplant, salt and pepper to taste, sausage, and cheeses, then repeat. Sprinkle top with grated Parmesan and oregano.

Bake in oven at 325 degrees for 25 minutes; if grilling, cook for 30 minutes over medium coals. Leave uncovered for half the cooking time.

Serves 6-8

Grilled Garlic Bread

1 large loaf Italian bread
1 stick butter, softened
1/4 C. Parmesan cheese, grated
1 clove garlic, minced
1 1/2 t. parsley flakes
1/2 t. dried dill
1/2 t. dried oregano

Cut bread into 3/4-inch slices. Mix butter with other ingredients and spread between slices.

Wrap loaf loosely in foil, securing at both ends. Place on grill for 10-12 minutes.

Serves 4-6

Bruno's Cheese Bread

2 C. sifted flour
2 t. baking powder
1 T. sugar
1/2 t. salt
1/4 C. butter
1 C. sharp cheddar cheese, grated
1 T. onion, grated
1 1/2 t. dried dill
3/4 C. milk
1 egg, slightly beaten

Sift flour, baking powder, sugar, and salt into large bowl. With a pastry blender, cut in butter until mixture resembles coarse crumbs. Stir in cheese, onion, and dill. Mix well.

Combine milk and beaten egg; pour into flour mixture. Stir quickly with a fork, just to moisten other ingredients. Pour into greased and floured loaf pan.

Bake at 350 degrees for 40-45 minutes. Let cool in pan for 10 minutes, then remove and serve warm.

Serves 4-6

Moonman's Sweet Potato Cornbread Muffins

1 large sweet potato (to yield 2 C. pulp)
1/2 lb. butter, melted
6 medium eggs, beaten
5 oz. brown sugar
1/2 t. baking soda
1 t. cinnamon
1 t. salt
1 C. evaporated milk
2 C. finely ground cornmeal

Boil sweet potato in its jacket, then peel. Puree pulp and add butter. Beat eggs with sugar, soda, cinnamon, and salt, then add to puree. Beat in evaporated milk and cornmeal.

Pour mixture into buttered 2 1/2-inch muffin tins and bake at 375 degrees until browned, about 30 minutes.

Makes 18 muffins

Baked Pineapple

2 (2 lb.) cans chunk pineapple
2 T. flour
3/4 C. sugar
1 t. salt
1 stick margarine
1/2 lb. Velveeta cheese, shredded
bread crumbs

Drain pineapple and reserve juice. In a saucepan, combine flour, sugar, salt, and margarine with pineapple juice and cook until mixture becomes thick. Add cheese and stir.

Pour mixture over pineapple chunks in a 2-quart casserole. Stir to coat pineapple. Top with dry bread crumbs and a pat of margarine.

Bake at 350 degrees for 20-25 minutes.

Serves 6-10

Kansas Dirt

1 large pkg. Oreo or Hydrox cookies, crushed
1 (8 oz.) pkg. cream cheese
1 stick butter
1 C. powdered sugar
3 C. milk
2 pkgs. instant vanilla pudding
1 t. vanilla
1 (12 oz.) carton of Cool Whip

Put half the crushed cookies in the bottom of 9 x 13-inch cake pan.

Cream together cream cheese, butter, and powdered sugar. Add milk, pudding, vanilla, and Cool Whip; blend well. Pour mixture over crushed cookies and top with other half.

Freeze or refrigerate until firm.

Serves 8-12

Apple Cake Pudding

3/4 C. sugar
1/4 C. butter
1 egg
1 C. flour
1 t. soda
1 t. cinnamon
1/2 t. nutmeg
1/4 t. coriander
4 C. apples, chopped
1 t. vanilla
1 C. nutmeats
cream (optional)

Cream together sugar, butter, and egg. Sift well the flour, soda, cinnamon, nutmeg, and coriander; blend into creamed mixture. Add remaining ingredients and stir into 1 1/2-quart casserole.

Bake at 350 degrees for 1 hour. Drizzle each serving with cream if desired.

Serves 6-8

Oatmeal Cake

1 C. oatmeal
1 1/4 C. boiling water
3/4 C. sugar
3/4 C. brown sugar
1/2 C. shortening
2 eggs
1 1/2 C. flour
1 t. soda
1/2 t. salt
1/2 t. nutmeg
1/2 t. cinnamon

Topping

1 C. coconut
2/3 C. brown sugar
1/2 C. nuts
6 T. melted butter
6 T. cream
1 t. vanilla

Mix oatmeal and boiling water. Cream together sugars, shortening, and eggs; stir into cooked oatmeal. In separate bowl, sift together flour, soda, salt, nutmeg, and cinnamon; add ingredients to oatmeal mixture.

Bake in 9 x 13-inch pan at 350 degrees for 35 minutes.

Combine topping ingredients and spread on cake. Put under broiler until brown.

Serves 6-8

Epilogue: Interviews with Excellence

What follows are a few suggestions, hints, methods, reminiscences, tips, and stories collected from some knowledgeable members of the Kansas City Barbeque Society. Each has unique credentials, and each has a personalized approach. These people *know* barbeque, and their comments will add flair to your quest for the Magic.

Paul Kirk (the Baron of Barbeque) is a chef by trade, who constantly experiments to improve his technique. He, like the other KCBS members interviewed, is a true aficionado and consistent contest winner.

Guy Simpson (The K.C. Rib Doctor) started his barbeque career as a hobby, eventually honing his technique to prizewinning form. Now he caters all kinds of events and, like the Baron, markets some of his unique barbeque spices.

Karen Putman proves that women are just as adept at barbeque as men. Being the only certified female executive chef in Missouri provides her a solid food background, which has contributed to the creativity she brings to barbeque.

Rich Davis has gained national prominence with his K.C. Masterpiece barbeque sauce and has recently opened a new, state-of-the-art restaurant in Kansas City.

The Schroeger brothers are 1987 Grand Champions with the KCBS. Their technique is based on methods handed down from their father and grandfather, both having had their own devoted followings.

Rick Welch is a margin-tallying man of the '80s, with a love of barbeque that resulted in his River City Products firm.

Mark Mooney is a recent convert to smoke cooking, with a heavy background in restaurants and restaurant design work.

Gary and Carolyn Wells started entering and winning contests in the 1970s and helped form the Kansas City Barbeque Society. Gary is the president at the time of this writing and officiates at numerous contests and functions. Carolyn is administrator and key spokesperson for the Society.

Alan Uhl has competed in a wide range of contests (he helped conceive the Great Lenexa Barbeque Battle) and has been instrumental in formulating many of the bylaws for the KCBS. Plus, his all-night "pig in a pit" is a real crowd pleaser.

Now the masters speak.

Paul Kirk: Baron of Barbeque

On woods and their uses:

"First, it's more important to keep that constant temperature—the humidity in there and the smoke in there—rather than the actual type of wood used."

"I've found that if you go straight hickory it's going to be bitter. Hickory's a very predominant smoke. I like cooking with oak, always have, and I've used straight oak and won contests with it."

"I use a lot of apple wood that gives what I'll say is a little sweeter smoke. Whether it does or not, in my mind it does."

"I'm not a fan of real green hickory or any wood. I'd just as soon have at least six months on it agewise—it burns a little better and still you get a good effect."

"When I use hickory and oak, I use a lot more oak. Otherwise, there's too much smoke flavor; it overpowers everything else."

On handy barbeque items to have:

"Something that'll help is a fire starter chimney, so you'll always have hot briquettes to put in when your fire starts to die down."

"Sauces shouldn't ever be a problem. Find a sauce or rub at the store and experiment with it. Read the ingredients; you can play around and then make your own."

Miscellaneous tips, including philosophy:

"I've used all types of marinades, I've used mops. I like the mop we use now—it's a bug sprayer, the big fire-extinguisher type (that's never been used to spray for bugs), and we just spray everything down. [I might use] beer, apple juice, coffee, all of the above—just depends."

"I experiment more than anyone. I've yet to go into a season with the same rub, the same sauce, the same anything. The procedure's all different each year."

"Sometimes we mop. I've injected, marinated—primarily I use a rub, and I think that's more the key than anything."

"A lot of people ask if I parboil ribs. There's nobody, well, very few of us, who will do that. But I've had people say, 'Well, I've parboiled for thirty years and my family just loves it . . .' Well, why change; it's successful. But don't be afraid to experiment a little, too."

———————

Guy Simpson: The K.C. Rib Doctor

On doing it correctly from the start:

"Learn your pit, whatever you're cooking on; know how it cooks. If you don't know how to operate it, learn. Learn how long 25-30 briquettes are going to last. Don't use a gas grill—you know how they work. You push a button, watch your face blow up, and fifteen minutes later dinner's done."

"For John Q. Public, using a common, inexpensive smoker that everyone can own and have some fun with—he should take an extra thirty dollars and buy a few gadgets that can make control of life much easier. Buy either throwaway aluminum poundcake pans or teflon-lined pans for water. Buy a candy thermometer that'll go up to 400 degrees. On the smoker, put the bottom vents wide open. You control all the temperature up above with those vents. . . . you stick that candy thermometer in there, and it'll get you to the right temperature and will let you know, when things drop 25 degrees or so, that it's time to lift the lid and drop in a few more briquettes and maybe some more chips. Don't trust any thermometer that comes on a smoker."

"When I started out—my first time—I fed that smoker for twelve hours with straight hickory, and it was so bad you couldn't eat it. Now I mix my woods and use a simple formula: the hickory log goes on the left, the charcoal's in the middle, and the oak log goes on the right. Just a few handfuls of chips of any flavor in, say, a Weber, will condense that flavor. . . ."

"The last thing you want to do is buy a cheap piece of meat."

Insights:

"The Baron hangs his ribs; they're not laying on the grill. Sometimes I roll them and secure 'em with a skewer, then put 'em upright on the grill. If you do this, you unroll them for the last thirty minutes and apply sauce (if you want sauce on 'em) and rotate them every five to ten minutes. I also use racks that stand them on edge as they're smoking."

"Get a logbook and write down what you do. That way, you make notes on what works and what needs to be tried next time. Don't trust your memory—it's the second thing to go."

"One of our old tricks was to take a pork loin and just roll it out, keep filleting it out like a jellyroll, and then fill it with seasonings and spices, roll it back up, tie it up, and put it in the pit."

"Too much sauce can wreck good barbeque. Often, the best way to eat barbeque is with no sauce."

"In some parts of the country, they'll smoke one thing—all beef in Texas, all pork in Arkansas, the Carolinas, that kind of thing. Here, we'll cook anything that moves; it'll end up sliding into a smoker."

Answers to two basic, critical questions by Paul Kirk, Baron of Barbeque, and Guy Simpson, the K.C. Rib Doctor:

Q: What's the basic description of Kansas City Barbeque?
A: (simultaneously) Sweet and hot.
Q: If you had to say "O.K., here's a temperature you can smoke virtually anything at and get good results," what would it be?
A: 220 degrees with light smoke and plenty of moisture.

Karen Putman: KCBS Female Power

On entering barbeque contests:

"I had no interest in barbeque. I was a chef. I got into it when one of my employees said he was going to enter a contest. He mentioned a 'booth award.' That was what I got interested in—he'd cook and I'd get that booth award. Doing the booth turned into feeding the public, which I like, and I like to put on a show. Later I got into the cooking. Now I go to all the contests. . . ."

"If I had my way, everybody'd win a ribbon. Winning ribbons and trophies are more important than winning money. You'll spend the money [but] you'll have the trophies and ribbons forever."

Some basic advice:

"When smoking, I go strictly with fruitwoods—no hickory, no mesquite. Apple's dominant, cherry, pecan . . . cherry's good with beef, especially. Apple's good with fish, or anything for that matter."

"I cook everything between 175 degrees and 200 degrees. If I'm in a hurry, 225 degrees once in a while."

"I use a dry rub on the ribs—it's a 'no rhyme or reason' rub. I'll go down my spice rack and throw in everything I've got—cinnamon, cloves, curry, anything and everything."

"A lot of people wrap meats in foil. You won't find any foil in my booth—I use Saran wrap. It keeps the moisture in and it keeps the heat in better than foil."

"We use charcoal to start our fire, then we go to straight wood. We use sterno to start the fire, not liquids—sterno burns longer and doesn't splatter."

"Keep your smoker *clean*. I take mine to the car wash before every contest. I clean it out totally. I can smoke chicken on a clean smoker and a dirty smoker and there's a *big* difference in taste. Also, the color of the meat will be different. A cleaner smoker gives a cleaner taste. Night and day."

"I've got a mop that I use on chicken that's instant coffee, wine vinegar, oregano (and I hate oregano), sugar, tomato—it's really thin, almost watery. I'll smoke for an hour, then mop every twenty minutes."

An award-winning salmon technique:

"We took whole salmon and then boned them out, and we pounded them out until they were paper-thin almost. Then we made a scallop mousse—it was just scallops, eggs, and heavy cream—and we did a plain scallop mousse, a saffron scallop mousse, and a parsley scallop mousse. So then we spread each layer out over the salmon and rolled it up. Of course, after we smoked it we'd cut into it and it looked just like a jellyroll. It's a wonderful tasting salmon hot or cold. We serve it on a lemon-dill sauce."

Rich Davis: Nationally Recognized Barbeque Expert

On Kansas City barbeque:

"I entered the first American Royal contest, but they wouldn't let me enter the amateur division since K.C. Masterpiece had gotten started by that time and was doing really well in Kansas City. So I was up against these huge, big smokers, all these restaurants, and I had my little water smoker—maybe eighteen inches in diameter—and we won first place in the commercial division with pork tenderloin. That's the only official barbeque contest I ever entered."

"Kansas City barbeque is primarily closed-pit and the primary wood is hickory. What's unusual about K.C. barbeque is that the quality of it is superior to most places in this country. Secondly are the numbers of kinds of foods that people here will barbeque. I've been to every city in the country that does barbeque, spent weeks and weeks, and other cities have some good barbeque, but no city has as many good barbeque restaurants or has as wide a variety of barbequed foods as K.C.—I mean, they just don't."

"You ask about a 'Kansas City' flavor? Well, the most famous Kansas City barbeque for decades was Arthur Bryant's. Bryant's sauce is like no other in this town. So if you're talking about a K.C. flavor, that's one. Then Ollie Gates was the second best known, for sure, and his sauce had more chili powder or cumin flavor. Then our 'original' [K.C. Masterpiece] came on and fits neither the Bryant nor the Gates profile. So K.C. really has several flavors."

On barbeque in general:

"I'm a traditionalist, which is neither good nor bad. I don't marinate much; I'm primarily a dry rub person. I really like a water smoker, and I like a rotisserie—I think a rotisserie leaves the meat much more moist. I don't like barbeque as dry as some people do."

"Historically, again neither good nor bad, men have been associated most often with barbeque. It's often a participatory event, and it's about the only cooking style that men have a serious grasp on. It's one of the few areas in which people participate, and it takes hours to do it. And because people spend so much time and a fair amount of money, they're going to have a real *hankering* about it. There's real personal involvement and personal committment with barbeque that's true of almost no other food or cooking style."

"We use only live woods, logs. Our closed pit is traditional hickory and our open grill is pecan. Hickory's right in the mid-range of smokes; pecan's lighter, a very low residue smoke."

"My favorite barbeque is always the barbeque I'm eating at that moment. I've tasted some bad barbeque in my day, but never by people who've liked it enough to make it a serious pastime."

One all-encompassing tip:

"Cook it low and cook it slow."

The Schroeger Brothers: A Family Tradition

How they do it:

"We don't mix up a dry rub and put it on the meat. We do each seasoning separately. We do them basically in order: first, light salt, to get the meat wet more than anything, and then pepper, garlic salt, Accent or MSG, and celery salt and paprika. Layer by layer, with the paprika last to hold the seasonings. We do variations for chicken, beef, and pork roast."

"We have basically stuck with hickory on everything. I do like apple wood for chicken. We've tried all the other woods, but we just stay with hickory because we think that's what barbeque's all about."

"We don't do any injecting—most of ours is seasonings and the sauce. We marinate brisket, then we season it, then a lot of smoke—heavy on the smoke. We don't marinate much other than brisket."

"We try to keep the temperature between 140 degrees and 180 degrees. We're heavy on the smoke early (we're more worried about the smoke early on then the heat); you gotta have heat of course, but we really hit it with the smoke."

"We don't use specialty cuts—baby backs you can buy at any supermarket, chicken breasts, pork loin, anything."

"A novice guy using a Weber, who just comes out and builds a fire, throws some hickory on it, puts the meat over water or off to the side, not directly over the coals, and leaves it for three and a half to four hours, never looks at it, he's going to have a good piece of meat. It'll be tender, done. But the more time and care put in on watching the meat and taking care of the meat—pampering it more or less—the better end product he'll get."

"The main thing with ribs is to keep the fire from getting too hot, and to keep turning 'em all the time so you get even smoke top and bottom. Whether you stack 'em, lay 'em straight out on a grill or use a rib rack, you still need to turn 'em so you get smoke from every direction. Pay attention to them."

Rick Welch: Sir Loin

Barbeque magnate:

It all started on a rainy afternoon at Arthur Bryant's BBQ and has now become a barbeque dynasty. Rick Welch has built a hobby of grilling steaks into one of the nation's largest clearinghouses for quality bbq spices, sauces, and seasonings.

"I've done it all, steaks, lamb, fish, on the grill, but I needed something more. I took my ability to sell and have made a very successful business out of my hobby. I love my job."

"Founding the Kansas City Barbeque Society was just a natural extension of attending barbeque contests and meeting a lot of truly great people."

Mark Mooney: "Moon Man"

On K.C. barbeque and a miraculous occurence:

"We moved here from up by Chicago in 1980, and it took about two hours and forty minutes to fall in love with smoked food. We moved in the spring. It was amazing, the aroma all around town with everybody cooking out, with all the restaurants—truly amazing."

"There are even competitions within neighborhoods here—you hear, 'Hey, Jim down at 4512 has the best barbeque in the block.' I've lived other places and it's nothing like this. Here, everybody does it; it's what people do on weekends."

"Barbeque's got to have constant attention to give halfway uniform results. The backyard guy can do it. An individual restaurant may do it. But you can't really mass-produce the really good stuff. I don't think barbeque would every be really franchisable."

Gary Wells: Father of the KCBS

On the origins of the KCBS:

"The original rule of the KCBS was that none of it would be taken seriously. The organization was founded on the premise of promoting barbeque and having fun. Don't let the contestants fool you for a minute, though; they *do* take their cooking seriously, and they are just as serious about having a good time. We used to cook at all the contests we could—we've been to Memphis, Cleveland, even Ireland barbequing—but there's no place like home. Since the KCBS has grown so much, most of our efforts are on the 'administrative' end; we help civic and charitable organizations organize and conduct their contests. Also, the contestants know that if the contest is KCBS sanctioned, uniform rules and judging procedures will be followed, the judging will be fair, and they won't have to wait 'til next Wednesday to find out who won. It does my heart good to see a bunch of happy cookers and it's a way of giving back to the community. I'm proud of what we've achieved and appreciate the vote of confidence the barbequers have in me and in the KCBS."

Carolyn Wells: Literary Entrepreneur

Hog wild for barbeque:

"I have always loved barbeque and became acquainted with barbeque contests as a sport in 1981. At the time, I was affiliated with a barbeque sauce company,

Wicker's, and had the opportunity to meet barbequers from all over the United States. We entered some contests and were fortunate enough to rack up a few ribbons. Of course, then we were hooked. One of my functions with the KCBS is to act as a barbeque information center—through our newsletter, *The Bullsheet,* as correspondent with the *Goat Gap Gazette,* and so on. Barbeque is the new food craze, and we are in the perfect place to promote it and spread the word. My love of 'que led to the co-founding of Pig Out Publications, publisher of barbeque cookbooks, and to writing a 'Southern-style' barbeque book, *Barbecue Greats— Memphis Style.*"

Alan Uhl: The Great Lenexa Barbeque Battler

On contests:

"We've come a long way. When we did our first contest—before the KCBS—we had a bunch of folks sitting on a hillside with calculators and Big Chief tablets tabulating results. Now we're computerized. We've also got a proclamation signed by the governor declaring that our contest is the state championship event."

"It's great to go to big competitions because you see so many different techniques and things being done that you don't see at the smaller ones."

On ability and personal preferences:

"I know people who say they can tell the difference in meat smoked over apple and cherry, peach and pear, oak, hickory, and sassafras. . . . I'm not that good, but I believe there are people who can do that."

"I do lamb about as well as anybody alive, speaking modestly."

"Once I started out with a stenographer's notebook to write down everything I did—what I did, so I could work on it—and it didn't pan out. I wouldn't do it. Now I decide what I'm going to do in a contest as I'm packing up and heading out. I won St. Joe last year, and what I put on those ribs was Creole seasoning I got at the store on the way, and I basted 'em with a mixture of Wicker's [marinade] and beer and some honey and maybe some apple juice—I can't remember."

"The great thing about barbeque is that you can do something totally opposite of what someone else says about marinades or rubs or sauces, and come out beautifully."

"Low and constant heat's the most important thing. That's why a lot of big, custom smokers are insulated now—to help maintain temperature. I think 225 degrees is best for any meat."

"When you're doing something that doesn't have any skin on it, or fat cover on it, wrap it in cheesecloth. I've done rabbits that've been terrific. The cloth helps hold the moisture, the marinade. I always wrap turkey breast in cheesecloth."

"One time I had the butcher save the long slabs of fat cut off prime ribs. Well, usually you cook a brisket fat side up, but I did this one fat side down with those layers, slabs of fat, on top. That was excellent."

"If the backyard Joe'll mix equal parts black pepper, garlic powder, paprika, and a little salt, and rub it into the meat, it'll be a good place to start."

An ambitious, crazed all-night pig in a pit:

"Remember when we did pig underground? We'd dig a pit four feet deep and four long and three wide, get half a cord of wood and burn all day. Then we'd fill an eighty-to-ninety pound pig up with cornstalks, or a couple of times I used a bunch of oranges and pineapples and stuff they'd squeezed to make juice at the super-market, and filled the pig up with that. Then we'd cover the pig all over with a pork rub, then wrap him in cheesecloth, then wrap him in chicken wire. Now I've got this bed of coals in the ground—more where we're gonna put the back of the pig (it has more meat)—and we cover the coals with a bunch of cornstalks. Then we'd put the pig in on top of that—and it's a pretty spectacular evening sight—and we'd cover it with more cornstalks, canvas, then a couple sheets of corrugated tin, then fill in the dirt and come back twelve hours later, dig him up and eat him. Great, just great."

The Kansas City Barbeque Society Roster

Mark Adams
Tom Adams
Karen Adler
Linda Aldridge
Skip Aldridge
Craig Alexander
David Ammon
Joseph C. Arnold
R. "Dick" Avard III
William Scott Ayres
Pat Baldridge
Jim Banner
Tricia Banner
Barbecue Industry
    Association
Karen Barksdale
Gary Barrett
Richard &
    Pam Beach
John Beadle
Perry Beal
Thomas R. Bean
Curt Bednar
Dale E. Bennett
Hon. Richard L.
    Berkley
Jerry Bicknell
Matt Bilardo
Billy Bones BBQ
Don Blackman
Martin & Cindy Blair
Al Bohnert
Chris Boland
Patrick A. Born
George H. Brewer
Bill Brown
Bob Brown
Kenny Brown
Phil Brown
Tom Byron

Russell Buchan
Terry Buchheit
Pam Buck
Gina & Larry
    Buckley
Jeffrey M. Burnett
Reith R. "Buz"
    Busby
James R. Calcara
Ronaldo Camargo
Joe Canavan
Larry Carden
Dick Corbo
    Catering
Jerry Catt
Peter J. Celliers
Deborah Chapman
Rebecca Christian
Doug & Lee Ann
    Cifer
Jerry Clark
Stephen J. Clifford
Michael J. Compton
Harold & Muriel
    Cook
Marlee Cooper
Ken Cormack
Bob Corn
Vern A. Coryell
Mike Coupe
Kenny Craig
Kirk "Sgt. Fro" Craig
John R. Craver
Andy Croughan
Rita Barber
    Cucchiara
Norther Cullins
Steve Culver
Bruce Daniel
Dale E. Darnell

Teresa & Fred
    Davidson
Ardie Davis
Dr. Rich Davis
Jack Dean
Ed Denault
Double E Bar-B-Q
Bob & Janet Douglas
Fred Douglas
Don Dowdall
Ken Downs
Gene G. Duckworth
Scott Durham
Chef John "Roscoe"
    Eddy
Kent Edmondson
Mike Edmondson
Vic Eiskina
Steve Eller
John Ellis
Gary Embry
Kansas City, Kansas,
    Community Col-
    lege Endowment
    Fund
Rod Engelland
Diana & Bill Ennis
Lori Erickson
Roger E. Evans
Larry G. Ewing
Tom Ferguson
Ken Fischer
Warren A. Fischer
Carl R. Fisher
Matt Fisher
Ron Fisher
Jim Flynn
Gary D. Ford
Larry Foster
Mary Frain

Ray H. France
Dixie Franklin
Frank's Country Inn
Fred J. Friend
Larry Fritsche
Jim Galle
Sonny & Dorrie
    Garren
Mickey Gist
Harley Goerlitz
Arturo Gonzalez
Paul Grahovac
Steven Grant
Jerry M. Greene
David R. Greig
Tom Groneman
Craig Haake
Dan Haake
Rick Haight
Smoky Hale
Tom "T-Bone" Hall
Randy Hamilton
Timothy Hamilton
John J. Hangley
Jim Hannah
Grace Harris
Libby Hayes
Pat Hayes
Mark E. Heckman
Brian Heiden
Mark A. Henry
Terry Henry
Mark Herring
Mike Herron
Donald Hickert
Tom Hickey
James L. Hicks
Martin Hintz
Kenneth Hobbs
Tim Hoelting

Tim Hoelting
Matt Hoey
Tom Hoffman
Steve Holbrook
Lee & Sonia Holt
Jim Houghton
Dan Howard
Bernard Howard, Sr.
Buzzy Hughes
Robert Hult
Gilbert Hunter
Don Hysko
Schulyer Ingle
Doug Irvin
John Jackson
Myron Jackson
Byron Jacobson
Glynda Jacobson
Harold E. Jansen
Charles Jean-
   Baptiste
Greg Johnson
Maurice Johnson
Jerry Joiner
Herman A. Jones, Jr.
Steve Katz
Jack R. Kay
Ronna Keck
John D. Kenney III
Craig Kidwell
Steve & Mary Ann
   Kingsford
Jessica Kirk
Paul Kirk
Sammie Knight
Larry G. Koch
Fred Kohnken
Eugene W. Kovar
John Kunick
Bob Kunze, Jr.
Art La Belle
Frosty Langdon
David Lawrence

W. Timothy
   Lawrence
Al Lawson
Bob J. Lawson
Ed Lawson
Millard Leach
Jeff W. Lee
Florence Lemkowitz
John Lillish
Keith Lindblom
Carl Lingo
Phil Litman
S. W. "Butch" Lloyd
Frank Lo Presti
Robert Lofaro
James C. Lollis, Jr.
Dwayne Looney
Cleo G. Lowry, Jr.
Jeff Lunceford
Bob Lyon
Adele Malott
Dennis Malotte
Larry Malotte
Gerry Markham
Bobbie Marks
John Martinez
Jim Massey
Cindy Mathews
Kent Maune
Dave McCabe
Dale McCloud
Bobby McGee
Mike McGonigle
Jeff McMains
Diana McMillan
Donna McClure
Ted McClure
Bill Melahn
Phil Melton
Beverly Metzger
Janeyce Michel
Fenton W. Miller, III
Ralph J. Mills

Ken Moberg
Sally Moore
Thomas Morcione
Daniel J. Morey
Robert Morse
Kevin Murphy
Neil Murphy
Murray Industrial
   Food Sales
Mustard's Restaurant
John H. Nichols
Stacey Niyamoto
Bubba Norris
Pam Norris
Scott O'Meara
Jan O'Neal
Mike O'Neill
Barbara W.
   Oringderff
Jim Oroke
Donnie J. Owens
Jerry Palmer
Cheryl Parker
Robert Pearsson
Bradley Pemberton
Rick Perkins
Erma Perry
Jeff Peterson
Herb Phillips
Charlie Podrebarac
Susan Pollack
Bill Powell
Maureen Powell
Larry Pratt
Joy & Steve Press
Jim Pryor
Donald L. Pugh
Jim Putman
Karen Putman
Jim Ragland
Bruce Ramage
Ian Ramage
Mike Ramage

Jim Ramey
John Raven
Janet Redding
Jim Reinert
Carl Reniker
Doris Reynolds
Carl Rice
David Richardson
Bill Reinschmidt
Acey Ringo–Ringo's
   BBQ
Jim Roberson
Rita Roberson
Tom Roberson
Bob Roberts
Ron Roberts
Bill Robinson
Tom Rogers
Ed Roith
Jeffrey D. Rosen
James Roth
Pete Rowland
Richard V. Rozman
David Russell
Skip & Maggie
   Russell
Joe Ruwart
Rene Ryan
Steve Sagaser
Joy Sample
Mark "Uncle Joon"
   Sanders
Bob Schaffer
Steven H. Scheuer
Christopher
   Schlesinger
John Schlosser
Mark Schroeger
Paul Schroeger
Herb Schwarz
Jim Scott
Edward Seaman
John Sharpe

Randy Sheek
Curtis Shepard
Ken Shopen
Art Siemering
Guy Simpson
Mary Beth Simpson
John Sinnett
Jerry Donovan Sipes
C. Byron Smith
Meg Smith
Charles T. Stauch
Kathy Stauch
Wynn Steinkamp
Chilton C. Strode
Ronald Surma
Joey B. R. Sutphen
Gaylord Swartz
James Tabb
Rick Tallon, DDS
George Tamblyn
Dennis Taylor
Eunice Teifer Juckett

Bill Tempel
Mieko Teratani
Alissa B. Tevis
Trent N. Tevis
Mike Thompson
Tommy Thompson
Tom Treccariche
Mike True
Mike Turnell
Dan Turner
Bill Tuttle
C. E. "Ol' Smokey"
    Tuttle
Doug Tuttle
Richard Tuttle
Philip W. Tyler
Alan Uhl
Carol S.
    Unkenholz
Randy Unkenholz
Steve Vasquez
David Veljacic

"Wild Bill"
    Venable III
Phil "Frito"
    Villanueva
Terry Vriezelaar
Eric Wagner
Roger L. Wagner
Harold T. Walker
Claire Walter
Bruce Warnemunde
Dick "Gleason"
    Waterman
Norman B. Waters
R. S. Weber
Rick Welch
Carolyn S. Wells
Gary R. Wells
Jeannie
    Westmoreland
Walt Westmoreland
Duke Wheeler
Larry D. Wheeler

Chuck Whipple
Cornell White
Greg White
Bob Whitefield
John Wilcott
Bob Williams
Jack Williams
Tammy Williams
Becky Wilson
Dan Wilson
Lewis Wilson
Judy Wimberly
Thayer Wine
Jeff & Julie Wolf
Randy Wolff
Brian Wyman
Jack York
Jerry Young
Bob Zaban
George Zahn
Mike Zarda
Clayton Zellers

Mail Order Product Information

Recipes in *The Passion of Barbeque* may include special sauces and marinades only available in the Kansas City area. To obtain information about any hard-to-find products, write to:

The Kansas City Barbeque Society
11514 Hickman Mills Drive
Kansas City, MO 64134

The following companies stock specialty Kansas City barbeque products:

The Best of Kansas City
6233 Brookside Plaza
Kansas City, MO 64113
(816) 333-7900

Catch Kansas City
608 West 48th Street
Kansas City, MO 64112
(816) 753-7221

Heartland Market at Crown Center
Professional Chef Store
2450 Grand Avenue, Suite 1
Kansas City, MO 64108
ATTN: Shopper Advisory
(816) 426-1175

Kansas Sampler
9548 Antioch
Overland Park, KS 66212
(913) 383-2920

Missouri Memories
Seville Square
500 Nichols Road
Kansas City, MO 64112
(816) 931-9174

River City Products, Inc.
P. O. Box 14406
Kansas City, MO 64152
(816) 472-4363

Glossary

Baby Back Ribs—the 13 smallest loin end ribs of a slab of pork ribs, the most tender ribs.

Bamboo Skewers—long pins of wood soaked in water prior to using for kebabs on the grill.

Banking Coals—stacking charcoal briquettes against the wall of the grill to one side in order to grill using the indirect cooking method.

Barbeque—to slowly cook meat/food over coals with aromatic woods in a covered cooker imparting smoke flavor.

Baste—to pour liquids such as stock, juice, oils, or marinades over meats while cooking to retain moisture and/or impart flavor.

Charcoal Chimney—a cylindrical metal container used to start charcoal fires without the use of petroleum products.

Closed Pit—a covered barbeque grill.

Dry Rub—a mixture of dry seasonings rubbed into meats prior to grilling or barbequeing.

Glaze—a finishing sauce applied to meats during the final 15 minutes of cooking.

Green Wood—usually refers to unseasoned hickory.

Grilling—cooking over a hot open fire.

Hardwood Charcoal Briquettes—most commonly made from hardwoods such as oak or hickory.

Hoi Sin Sauce—also known as Chinese bean sauce, it is sweet and hot, made primarily from black beans.

Indirect Heat—to cook meat away from the source of heat, i.e., the opposite side of the grill away from the hot coals.

Indoor Barbequeing—cooking in the oven by broiling under a red hot heating unit or slow covered cooking in the oven using barbeque sauce or liquid smoke to imitate outdoor barbequeing.

Injecting Marinades—using a syringe with a needle to insert marinade into meats prior to cooking.

KCBS Sanctioned Contests—contests that apply for and follow the Kansas City Barbeque Society's criteria, rules and regulations.

Mad Dog—insane canine . . . moniker for the co-founder of the KCBS.

Marinate—to place food in an oil-acid mixture to tenderize or add flavor.

Mop—to use a mop or large brush to apply baste to meat while cooking.

Nom de Grille—imaginative names used by individuals or teams who compete in barbeque contests, i.e., The Rib Doctor, Baron of Barbeque, Sir Loin, Grill of my Dreams, to name a few.

Pit Barbeque—a large structure for barbequeing large pieces of meat or whole animals that can be closed for smoking. The pit can be a hole dug in the ground or a freestanding cement or brick "oven" or a heavy metal structure such as a metal drum.

Pit Boss—person in charge of the barbeque unit.

Sear—to brown quickly over a very hot charcoal fire to seal in meat juices.

Skewer—a long pin of wood or metal on which food is threaded/placed and held in place while cooking. To fasten meat with skewers to keep in shape while cooking.

Slab of Ribs—most commonly refers to pork ribs (a side or slab of ribs).

Waterpan—a vessel for water placed inside covered barbeque units to provide moisture while cooking.

Water Smoker—commercially manufactured cooking unit where the fire is separated from the meat by a water tray.

Wood—large chunks of non-resinous wood used as a fuel source as well as a smoke-flavoring agent. Varieties of woods used for barbequeing include: apple, cherry, grape, hickory, mesquite, oak, and pecan.

Wood Chips—small chips of hardwood or fruitwood added to barbeque fire to impart smoke flavor to meats.

Index by Cuts of Meat